THE COMPLETE BABY FOOD

Cookbook

500 Super Easy Wholesome Homemade Baby-Led Recipes For Every Age And Stage With Meal Plans For First-Time Parents

Lucia L. Davis

Table of Contents

Introduction

Babies are our little angels. Their smiles bring joy and enlighten our homes. From the first time you welcome them to your home, you want to love, care for, and protect them. Seeing them clean, healthy, and bubbly makes you a happy parent. If your baby refuses to eat some of the foods you prepare or does not eat at all, it's challenging. We understand this, and we are here for you. If you are struggling, you've found the best book to answer your questions. How great is it to understand your baby's feeding habits and how to deal with them? We provide different recipes to prepare nutritious and tasty foods for your little angel. Are you a first-time parent? We understand the excitement. Our cookbook is the answer to a smooth parenting journey. Please come with us.

Chapter 1
Essential Baby Food Information

Basics for Baby-Led Weaning

If you have decided to take this approach with your baby, you should understand a few important things. We are here to help you and your baby as we care about your child's development. Isn't our cookbook amazing? We would like to walk you through what to feed your baby during this period. It is important to understand what foods are or are not recommended. When your baby is ready for baby-led weaning, it can pick up small pieces of food. The recommended foods for this approach include but are not limited to avocado, eggs, melon slices, tofu, meat and fish, apples, sweet potatoes, and oats. Avocado is a highly nutritious food. In the first year, the baby grows rapidly, and it needs nutrition to aid in its growth. Place small pieces of avocado on your baby's plate or any other recommended foods, such as a banana or melon and it will self-feed. It's great to watch your child start this journey. Introduce your baby to foods rich in fiber, which helps boost their brain. Ensure eggs are fully cooked to avoid poisoning from salmonella exposure. Understanding what not to feed your baby is also critical. Avoid honey and corn syrup for babies under the age of one year as they may contain harmful bacteria that can cause paralysis in babies. You should also avoid foods that could choke your babies, such as sticky foods, raw foods, hard-to-chew foods, and coin-shaped foods. You shouldn't feed your baby unsafe liquids such as cow's milk, especially under one year because their digestive system isn't ready to process it. The age of your baby will determine how you prepare the food.

What is Baby-Led Weaning?

Does this sound familiar? Baby-led weaning is an approach that focuses on introducing solid food to a baby to complement breast milk or infant formula. This approach facilitates the baby's oral motor development, bolus formation and positive eating. The baby eats as much as it wants without you inserting a lot of food into its mouth or being forced to eat. The baby controls its feeding. It is an interactive session for the baby to enjoy family mealtimes. Unlike the traditional spoon feeding, where parents use a spoon to feed puréed food, the child is given pieces of food it can hold, which it can pick up and explore. In simple terms, this feeding approach is led by the baby, self-feeding. The toddler begins by holding, sucking, and licking the food before it gets to the stage where it can start eating it. This weaning approach doesn't mean you should stop breastfeeding your baby, rather the approach is aimed at introducing different things to the baby, such as texture, exploring tastes, smells and colors and deciding which suits. This is an important stage for your baby that shouldn't be rushed. You can start baby-led weaning at six months or as early as five months if your baby starts reaching for food.

Benefits of Homemade Baby Food

The excitement of being a first-time parent or the fact that you are starting baby-led weaning could be overwhelming, and you might end up making mistakes and feeding your baby that food you order from your favorite restaurant. Do you know how safe these restaurant foods are for your baby who isn't yet ready to digest solid foods? We want to show you the importance of homemade food. These benefits include:

- Less processed, homemade meals are easy for your baby to adapt to. Food in jars has a lot of starch and other ingredients to preserve it, but it lacks flavor. Being able to explore flavors is an important developmental stage.
- Nutritious and delicious. Processed foods are heated at very high temperatures to kill bacteria. This means that the food losses all its nutrients. With homemade meals, you use fresh ingredients and have the option to add any other ingredients to suit your child's needs. How does a homemade avocado and banana Purée sound?
- Alternatives. By now, you may have realized that food in jars tastes the same as they must meet certain standards. If you buy a jar of baby bolognese today, it wouldn't taste any different if you were to buy it tomorrow. With homemade meals, it will always be different. Homemade means your baby will have a slightly different taste and texture even if given the same dish daily limiting boredom.
- Saves time. As you prepare food for the rest of the family, you also prepare the baby's food. This saves time and energy.
- Cost-effective. Homemade baby food helps you say goodbye to long receipts. For the amount it costs to buy a single jar Purée, you could make six jars in the comfort of your home.

Foods to Avoid in the First Year

- Salty foods. Babies shouldn't be fed salty foods at this age. Salty foods are not good for the kidneys. Avoid adding salt or stock cubes when preparing food as they are high in salts. Avoid the following foods: bacon, crisps, crackers, and takeaways. You can control salts by making homemade meals.
- Sugars. Avoiding sugary foods and drinks protects the baby from tooth decay.
- Honey. It contains bacteria which could harm the baby's intestines. The bacteria produce toxins in the stomach leading to a serious illness known as botulism. Honey is considered a sugar, and therefore it also will cause tooth decay.

- Saturated fats. This fat could raise cholesterol levels which increase the chances of heart disease.
- Raw and slightly cooked eggs. Undercooked eggs could cause poisoning from salmonella exposure.
- Rice drinks. It would be best if you didn't give your child rice drinks as an alternative to breast milk as it could contain arsenic which is not good.
- Whole nuts, peanuts and other hard, sticky, or crunchy foods. These types of foods can easily choke your baby, so it is best to avoid them.
- Cow's milk. For babies under one, it will cause constipation and a sore tummy.

Potential Allergies

Introducing solid foods to a baby could cause an allergic reaction. The following are symptoms of a baby-led weaning allergy:

- Vomiting or diarrhea
- Swollen lips or throat
- Red and itchy eyes
- Blocked nose
- Rash or itchy skin
- Shortness of breath
- Cough

Some potential allergies or flare-ups include eczema, asthma, and hay fever, amongst others. If your family has a history of these conditions, you should see your doctor before introducing your baby to certain foods. If your baby has been diagnosed with these allergies, avoid foods that could trigger the allergy, some of which could be life-threatening; therefore, be careful.

Tackle Baby Pickiness

Introducing solid foods could be intimidating for you as a parent and it is disappointing to see your baby refuse to eat your prepared food. Allow us to show you how to overcome this challenge.

- Praise your child when it eats as this will make it feel good about food, and it will be looking forward to eating. If you criticize your baby for not eating, it will eventually refuse to eat.
- Properly present your food. Babies love attractive colors. How you present your food will determine whether it will eat it. Make sure you slice the food into attractive shapes.
- Set a good example by what you eat. Children learn through interaction. If you do not like a certain type of food, the baby won't like it either.
- Respect its appetite. Don't force your baby to eat and if it doesn't want to eat now, then understand it might eat later.
- Have a routine. Have a timetable for feeding your baby and what you will feed it. A plan will psycholog prepare the baby for mealtimes, and it will enjoy the food.
- Be patient with new foods. It takes time for the baby to adjust to new foods so avoid rushing new flavors and textures.
- Be creative. You should come up with ideas to make your baby's food interesting by improving the taste and preparing the food the way the baby likes it.
- Give your child options to choose from.

Understanding your baby's needs is the best gift for a parent and the child. It is fulfilling to see your baby enjoy the meals you have prepared for it and watching it grow. We will walk with you through this journey. We have gone through the hard work to make easy recipes in your kitchen. You also do not require a whole colony of utensils. You will not regret getting this book for yourself. Please relax and enjoy as we bring you life-changing recipes. Take another look at your baby's smile and walk straight to your kitchen to bless your baby with an amazing dish today. Have fun!

Chapter 2
Single- ingredient Purées(4-6 Months)

At this stage, the point is to introduce the baby to its first solid food. Your baby is ready for solids when it can hold its head up and sit upright, has doubled birth weight, and can close its mouth around a spoon. The Purée should be a very thin consistency with no chunkiness. Prepare the food so that it is easy for the baby to swallow. Purée is usually a single ingredient to help the parent identify any potential allergic reactions. It also helps the child identify different flavors and textures. Apart from feeding your baby with one ingredient, Purée, feed your baby with one type of Purée for four to five days, and then change it after that to another Purée. Consistency helps assess for any allergic reaction. Some of the Purées recommended at this stage include Puréed vegetables, fruits, meat and small amounts of unsweetened yogurt. Feed one to two teaspoons of Purée with 6 to 8 ounces of breast milk or formula. Increase the amount of Purée gradually. It is also critical to understand what not to feed your baby. For example, cow milk, salty and spicy foods, sticky and hard foods. The following are nutritional requirements at this stage:

- Vitamin D. Breast milk and infant formula are the primary source of nutrition, and this should be continued even though the baby is introduced to solid foods.
- Iron and Zinc. Iron and zinc in the baby's liver could run low, so it is important to feed it food rich in iron and zinc.

Awesome Applesauce

Applesauce was one of my baby's very first tastes of solid food. You might be worried that if you offer fruits first, it will spoil your baby's relationship with vegetables. This is simply not true, so offer this naturally sweet and delicious Purée to your baby with confidence.

Prep time: 5 minutes | Cook time: 10 minutes | Makes 16 (1-ounce) freezer cubes | Serving size: 2 tablespoons (1 cube)

- 4 medium apples, cored, peeled, and coarsely chopped (about 1½ pounds)
- ¼ teaspoon ground cinnamon (optional)

1. In a medium saucepan with a steamer basket or insert, bring about 1 inch of water to a simmer. Add the apples. Cover and simmer over low heat for 7 to 10 minutes, or until the apples are soft.
2. Remove from the heat and transfer the apples to a blender or food processor. Add the cinnamon (if using). Blend until smooth, adding a few tablespoons of water as needed to achieve your desired consistency.
3. Cool and serve, refrigerate in an airtight container for up to 3 days, or transfer to an ice cube tray and freeze for up to 3 months.

Creamy Avocado Purée

Avocados are fruits. Really? Avocado as a first food isn't strange. Avocados were one of my daughter's first foods since they are safe, quick to cook, and rich of healthy fats that are wonderful for brain development.

Prep time: 5 minutes | Cook time: 10 minutes | Makes 16 (1-ounce) freezer cubes | Serving size: 2 tablespoons (1 cube)

- 3 ripe avocados, pitted (about 1 pound)

1. Scoop the avocado flesh into a medium bowl. Discard the skins. Use a fork or potato masher to mash the avocado until smooth.
2. Serve immediately, refrigerate in an airtight container for up to 3 days, or transfer to an ice cube tray and freeze for up to 3 months.

Peanut Buttery Purée

New research recommends introducing common allergies, like peanuts, early and regularly. Relax! Start small. Give your baby a small scoop of this Purée and wait 10 to 15 minutes.

Prep time: 5 minutes | Cook time: 10 minutes | Makes 16 (1-ounce) freezer cubes | Serving size: 2 tablespoons (1 cube)

- ⅔ cup creamy, unsalted natural peanut butter
- 1⅓ cups breast milk, formula, or water

1. In a small bowl, combine the peanut butter with the breast milk, formula, or water. Mix until well combined.
2. Serve immediately, refrigerate in an airtight container for up to 3 days, or transfer to an ice cube tray and freeze for up to 3 months.

Juicy Blueberry Purée

Antioxidants like vitamin C found in blueberries improve absorption of iron and fiber for your baby. Use fresh or frozen blueberries for this dish. If you want sugar-free options, look for those.

Prep time: 5 minutes | Cook time: 5 minutes | Makes 16 (1-ounce) freezer cubes | Serving size: 2 tablespoons (1 cube)

- 4 cups fresh blueberries

1. In a medium saucepan with a steamer basket or insert, bring about 1 inch of water to a simmer. Add the blueberries. Cover and simmer over low heat for 3 to 5 minutes, or until the blueberries are soft.
2. Remove from the heat and transfer the blueberries to a blender or food processor. Blend until smooth, adding a few tablespoons of water as needed to achieve your desired consistency.
3. Cool and serve, refrigerate in an airtight container for up to 3 days, or transfer to an ice cube tray and freeze for up to 3 months.

Cool Carrot Purée

Most kids like carrots. Carrots are a delicious veggie that babies will likely prefer for years. Baby absorbs more beta-carotene from Puréed carrots. Baby carrots are a choking hazard and shouldn't be given to children under 4 years old.

Prep time: 5 minutes | Cook time: 15 minutes | Makes 16 (1-ounce) freezer cubes | Serving size: 2 tablespoons (1 cube)

- 5 medium carrots, peeled and coarsely chopped (about 1 pound)
- ½ cup water

1. In a medium saucepan with a steamer basket or insert, bring about 1 inch of water to a simmer. Add the carrots. Cover and simmer over low heat for 10 to 15 minutes, or until the carrots are soft.
2. Remove from the heat and transfer the carrots to a blender or food processor. Blend until smooth, adding ½ cup water (plus more as needed) to achieve your desired consistency.
3. Cool and serve, refrigerate in an airtight container for up to 3 days, or transfer to an ice cube tray and freeze for up to 3 months.

Superfood Spinach Purée

Spinach Purée may not seem delicious, but it's great for babies. Pair it with sweet fruits and vegetables like Juicy Blueberry Purée or Berry Green Smoothie. Whole leafy greens can suffocate young children. Purée leafy greens like spinach so your kid can still benefit from them.

Prep time: 5 minutes | Cook time: 5 minutes |Makes 16 (1-ounce) freezer cubes | Serving size: 2 tablespoons (1 cube)

- 1 (16-ounce) bag fresh spinach leaves

1. In a medium saucepan with a steamer basket or insert, bring about 1 inch of water to a simmer. Add the spinach. Cover and simmer over low heat for 3 to 5 minutes, or until the spinach has wilted.
2. Remove from the heat and transfer the spinach to a blender or food processor. Blend until smooth, adding a few tablespoons of water as needed to achieve your desired consistency.
3. Cool and serve, refrigerate in an airtight container for up to 3 days, or transfer to an ice cube tray and freeze for up to 3 months.

Nourishing Quinoa Cereal

My kids usually eat quinoa, but I didn't know about it until my late 20s. Quinoa is healthy. It's one of the few plant-based complete protein sources and contains heart-healthy lipids for baby's brain development. Plus, KEEN-wah sounds cool.

Prep time: 5 minutes | Cook time: 20 minutes |Makes 16 (1-ounce) freezer cubes | Serving size: 2 tablespoons (1 cube)

- ½ cup quinoa, rinsed
- 1½ cups water, divided

1. In a small saucepan, combine the quinoa and 1 cup water and bring to a boil over medium heat. Reduce the heat to low, cover, and cook for 10 to 15 minutes, or until all the water is absorbed. Turn off the heat and let sit, covered, for 5 additional minutes.
2. Transfer the quinoa to a blender or food processor. Blend until smooth, adding the remaining ½ cup water (plus more as needed) to achieve your desired consistency.
3. Cool and serve, refrigerate in an airtight container for up to 3 days, or transfer to an ice cube tray and freeze for up to 3 months.

Easy Chicken Purée

Chicken, especially dark meat, is a good source of iron when introducing meals to your kid. Try this simple Purée recipe with your baby and add more ingredients as you feel comfortable (for example, Chicken and Carrot Purée).

Prep time: 5 minutes | Cook time: 10 minutes |Makes 16 (1-ounce) freezer cubes | Serving size: 2 tablespoons (1 cube)

- 3 boneless, skinless chicken thighs, cut into 1-inch pieces (about ¾ pound)
- ½ cup water

1. In a medium saucepan with a steamer basket or insert, bring about 1 inch of water to a simmer. Add the chicken. Cover and simmer over low heat for 7 to 10 minutes, or until the chicken is cooked through and a thermometer registers 165°F.
2. Remove from the heat and transfer the chicken to a blender or food processor. Blend until smooth, adding ½ cup of water (plus more as needed) to achieve your desired consistency.
3. Cool and serve, refrigerate in an airtight container for up to 3 days, or transfer to an ice cube tray and freeze for up to 3 months.

Berry Blast Smoothie

Fruit is nature's candy. Your baby will love this delicious, nutritious mixture. This recipe can be used as a Purée, in an open or straw cup for practice, or as a teething popsicle.

Prep time: 5 minutes | Cook time: 10 minutes |Makes 32 (1-ounce) freezer cubes | Serving size: ¼ cup (2 cubes)

- 6 cups fresh or frozen mixed berries (blueberries, raspberries, strawberries, blackberries)
- 1 cup water

1. Add the berries and water to a blender or food processor. Blend until mostly smooth, adding a few tablespoons of water as needed to achieve your desired consistency.
2. Serve immediately, refrigerate in an airtight container for up to 3 days, or transfer to an ice cube tray and freeze for up to 3 months.

Eat Your Broccoli Purée

When it was time to give my daughter broccoli, I was excited. I hoped she'd adore it as much as I did because I knew she would. If your infant doesn't like a food you prepare, don't take it personally. This takes time and exposures. Keep trying! Use frozen steamed broccoli to save time. It's fresh-tasting.

Prep time: 5 minutes | Cook time: 10 minutes |Makes 12 (1-ounce) freezer cubes | Serving size: 2 to 4 tablespoons (1 or 2 cubes)

- 2 cups broccoli florets, roughly chopped (about 1 large head)
- 1 tablespoon unsalted butter or coconut oil
- ¼ to ½ cup water

1. Cover the bottom of a medium saucepan with 2 to 3 inches of water and bring it to a simmer over medium heat.
2. Put the broccoli into a steamer basket or stainless-steel colander and set it over the simmering water. Steam until bright and tender, 5 to 7 minutes. Keep a close eye on it so that it doesn't overcook (when it is overcooked, it will turn an olive-green color).
3. Put the broccoli into a blender along with the butter. Pour in ¼ cup water and blend, adding more water, 1 tablespoon at a time, as needed to reach your desired consistency.
4. Cool and serve, refrigerate in a sealed container for up to 3 days, or transfer to an ice cube tray and freeze for up to 3 months.

Quick Black Bean Purée

Beans, amazing fruit—wait! Beans are legumes, not fruits. Beans are nutrition magicians. They're full of iron, a crucial vitamin for your kid, and fiber to help during constipation. Vitamin C from lime juice helps iron absorption.

Prep time: 5 minutes | Cook time: 5 minutes |Makes 12 (1-ounce) freezer cubes | Serving size: 2 to 4 tablespoons (1 or 2 cubes)

- 1 (15-ounce) can low-sodium black beans, drained and rinsed
- 2 tablespoons olive oil
- ½ teaspoon ground cumin (optional)
- Freshly ground black pepper

1. Combine the beans, olive oil, cumin (if using), and pepper in a blender and pulse a few times, until well combined but still chunky. Alternately, mash the mixture with a fork until combined but still chunky.
2. Serve immediately, refrigerate in a sealed container for up to 3 days, or transfer to an ice cube tray and freeze for up to 3 months.

Oat-Alicious Cereal

Many newborns start with rice cereal, but it's not necessary. Arsenic in brown rice worries many parents. Oatmeal calms the mind. Whole-grain oatmeal is protein-rich and iron-fortified. You can also use breast milk or formula in this recipe.

Prep time: 5 minutes | Cook time: 5 minutes |Makes 16 (1-ounce) freezer cubes | Serving size: 2 tablespoons (1 cube)

- ½ cup old-fashioned rolled oats
- 2 cups water

1. In a food processor or blender, pulse the oats until you have a fine powder/flour.
2. In a medium saucepan, combine the oat flour and water and bring to a boil over medium heat. Cook, stirring frequently, for 3 to 5 minutes, or until bubbly and thick. For a thinner consistency, add more water a few tablespoons at a time. For a thicker consistency, continue to cook, stirring frequently.
3. Cool and serve, refrigerate in a sealed container for up to 3 days, or transfer to an ice cube tray and freeze for up to 3 months.

Easy Peasy Purée

Peas are a legume that's full in iron, protein, and other vitamins and minerals. For good reason, they're a classic starter. Choose frozen peas over canned. This will keep your baby's diet sodium-free.

Prep time: 5 minutes | Cook time: 10 minutes |Makes 16 (1-ounce) freezer cubes | Serving size: 2 tablespoons (1 cube)

- 1 (13-ounce) package frozen green peas
- ½ cup water

1. In a medium saucepan with a steamer basket or insert, bring about 1 inch of water to a simmer. Add the peas. Cover and simmer over low heat for 7 to 10 minutes, or until the peas are heated through.
2. Remove from the heat and transfer the peas to a blender or food processor. Blend until smooth, adding ½ cup of water (plus more as needed) to achieve your desired consistency.
3. Cool and serve, refrigerate in a sealed container for up to 3 days, or transfer to an ice cube tray and freeze for up to 3 months.

My Sweet Lil' Potato Purée

often prescribe sweet potatoes to caregivers. Their flavor and nutrients are hard to beat. If you don't have time to roast the potatoes, stab them with a fork and microwave them until soft.

Prep time: 5 minutes | Cook time: 45 minutes |Makes 16 (1-ounce) freezer cubes | Serving size: 2 tablespoons (1 cube)

- 2 medium sweet potatoes (about 1 pound)
- ½ cup water

1. Preheat the oven to 425°F. Line a rimmed baking sheet with aluminum foil or parchment paper.
2. Prick the sweet potatoes all over with a fork. Place the sweet potatoes on the prepared baking sheet and bake for about 45 minutes, or until soft.
3. Remove from the oven and let cool slightly. Use a spoon to scoop the cooked sweet potato flesh into a medium bowl. Use a fork or potato masher to mash the sweet potato until smooth, adding ½ cup of water (plus more as needed) to achieve your desired consistency.
4. Cool and serve, refrigerate in a sealed container for up to 3 days, or transfer to an ice cube tray and freeze for up to 3 months.

Peach Purée

This Pear Purée is like Applesauce, but more complex. Vanilla adds sweetness and warmth. I recommend ripe Anjou, Bartlett, or Comice pears. Most pears at the supermarket are hard, so ripen them on your counter until the narrow section gives when you press on it.

Prep time: 10 minutes | Cook time: 1 minute|Makes 16 (1-ounce) freezer cubes | Serving size: 2 tablespoons (1 cube)

- 4 medium peaches (about 1½ pounds)

1. Bring a large pot of water to a boil. Place the peaches in the boiling water and cook for 30 seconds.
2. Using a slotted spoon, remove the peaches and transfer to a bowl of ice water. Let the peaches cool slightly, then use your hands to gently rub the skin off. Remove the pits and coarsely chop the peaches.
3. Transfer the peaches to a blender or food processor. Blend until smooth, adding a few tablespoons of water as needed to achieve the desired consistency.
4. Cool and serve, or transfer to an ice cube tray and freeze.

Prune Purée

This Peach Purée will remind your infant of summer. You may feed your infant frozen peach slices even in winter. Microwave 4 cups frozen peach slices and combine with liquids until smooth. Peaches contain vitamin A for good eyesight and vitamin C to boost your baby's immune system.

Prep time: 5 minutes, plus 20 minutes to soak|Makes 16 (1-ounce) freezer cubes | Serving size: 2 tablespoons (1 cube)

- 1½ cups pitted prunes

1. Put the prunes in a medium heat-safe bowl. Pour boiling water over the prunes to cover. Soak for 15 to 20 minutes, or until the prunes soften.
2. Strain the prunes, reserving the liquid, and transfer the prunes to a blender or food processor. Blend until smooth, adding 1 cup of the soaking liquid (plus more as needed) to achieve the desired consistency.
3. Cool and serve, or transfer to an ice cube tray and freeze.

Blueberry Purée

My young girl loved blueberries. Blueberries are high in vitamin C and antioxidants, which help protect cells. Blueberries are a summer fruit, so they're best then. In winter, frozen blueberries are best. Instead of boiling frozen berries, microwave them and combine with juices.

Prep time: 5 minutes | Cook time: 5 minutes|Makes 16 (1-ounce) freezer cubes | Serving size: 2 tablespoons (1 cube)

- 4 cups fresh blueberries

1. In a medium saucepan with a steamer basket or insert, bring about 1 inch of water to a simmer. Add the blueberries. Cover and simmer over low heat for 3 to 5 minutes, or until the blueberries are soft.
2. Remove from the heat and transfer the blueberries to a blender or food processor. Blend until smooth, adding a few tablespoons of water as needed to achieve the desired consistency.
3. Cool and serve, or transfer to an ice cube tray and freeze.

Mango Purée

Mango Purée is sweet and creamy, making it a baby favorite. Mangos contain vitamins A and C. Vitamin B6 helps your baby grow. 1 (15-ounce) bag of frozen mango chunks can be microwaved and combined with juices. Mango Purée goes well with cereal, yogurt, legumes, and avocado.

Prep time: 10 minutes | Cook time: 5 minutes|Makes 16 (1-ounce) freezer cubes | Serving size: 2 tablespoons (1 cube)

- 3 mangos, pitted, peeled, and coarsely chopped (about 1½ pounds)

1. In a medium saucepan with a steamer basket or insert, bring about 1 inch of water to a simmer. Add the mangos. Cover and simmer over low heat for 3 to 5 minutes, or until the mangos are soft.
2. Remove from the heat and transfer the mangos to a blender or food processor. Blend until smooth, adding a few tablespoons of water as needed to achieve the desired consistency.
3. Cool and serve, or transfer to an ice cube tray and freeze.

Green Pea Purée

Green peas have the taste of a vegetable yet the nourishment of a bean. Green peas are a legume, thus they're high in iron and protein. Babies enjoy their natural sweetness. Frozen peas are cheaper and easier to use than fresh, shelled peas in this recipe.

Prep time: 5 minutes | Cook time: 10 minutes|Makes 16 (1-ounce) freezer cubes | Serving size: 2 tablespoons (1 cube)

- 1 (13-ounce) package frozen green peas
- ½ cup water

1. In a medium saucepan with a steamer basket or insert, bring about 1 inch of water to a simmer. Add the peas. Cover and simmer over low heat for 7 to 10 minutes, or until the peas are heated through.
2. Remove from the heat and transfer the peas to a blender or food processor. Blend until smooth, adding ½ cup of water (plus more as needed) to achieve the desired consistency.
3. Cool and serve, or transfer to an ice cube tray and freeze.

Easy Green Pea Purée

If you don't want to shell fresh peas, buy frozen; they're just as healthy. Peas must be boiled before Puréeing, especially if the Purée will be frozen, to prevent harmful germs from developing.

Prep time: 5 minutes| Cook time: 5 minutes| Serves 6 (¼-CUP)

- 1 (10-ounce) bag frozen peas

1. In a medium saucepan over medium heat, bring ⅓ cup of water to a gentle boil. Add the peas and simmer for 2 minutes.
2. Remove the peas, reserving the cooking water, and allow the peas to cool slightly. Carefully transfer the peas and cooking water to a food processor. Purée until smooth, pausing to scrape down any larger pieces from the sides of the bowl.

Easy Butternut Squash Purée

Roasting butternut squash gives a caramelized exterior. This procedure also works for acorn squash and sweet pumpkins.

Prep time: 5 minutes| Cook time: 60 minutes| Serves 12 (¼-CUP)

- 1 medium butternut squash (about 3 pounds)

1. Preheat the oven to 375°F degrees. Line a large, rimmed baking sheet with parchment paper. (This will help with cleanup.)
2. Rinse the squash under running water and pat dry. Use a large, sharp knife to cut the squash in half lengthwise. Scoop out the seeds with a spoon. Place the squash halves cut-side down on the baking sheet and pour water into the pan until the pan is half full. (To prevent spills, you may want to do this step once the baking sheet is already in the oven.)
3. Bake the squash for 40 minutes to 1 hour, until the skin puckers and the squash is easily pierced with a fork. Carefully remove the baking sheet from the oven, using extra care to avoid any water spills.
4. Allow the squash to cool for 10 to 15 minutes. Then, scoop the cooked squash out of the skin, transfer it to a food processor, and Purée until smooth, pausing to scrape down any larger pieces from the sides of the bowl.

Sweet Potato Purée

If the orange color doesn't captivate your baby, the sweet flavor and fluffy texture will. Sweet potatoes are plenty of fiber, vitamin A, and potassium to strengthen baby's muscles and blood pressure. If you have time, roasting sweet potatoes is easier than steaming them.

Prep time: 5 minutes | Cook time: 45 minutes | Makes 16 (1-ounce) freezer cubes | Serving size: 2 tablespoons (1 cube)

- 2 medium sweet potatoes (about 1 pound)
- ½ cup water

1. Preheat the oven to 425°F. Line a rimmed baking sheet with aluminum foil or parchment paper.
2. Prick the sweet potatoes all over with a fork. Place the sweet potatoes on the prepared baking sheet and bake for about 45 minutes, or until soft.
3. Remove from the oven and let cool slightly. Use a spoon to scoop the cooked sweet potato flesh into a medium bowl. Use a fork or potato masher to mash the sweet potato until smooth, adding ½ cup of water (plus more as needed) to achieve the desired consistency.
4. Cool and serve, or transfer to an ice cube tray and freeze.

Apple Purée

Apple varietal affects Purée flavor. Sweet Galas, sharp Granny Smiths, and acidic Jazz apples. Create a personalized Purée for your baby by combining different types.

Prep time: 5 minutes | Cook time: 10 minutes | Serves 5 (¼-cup)

- 1 pound (about 3 medium) apples

1. Fill a saucepan halfway with water. Set a steamer basket in the pan and place the pan over medium heat.
2. Rinse the apples under running water and pat dry. Peel and core the apples, then cut them into 1-inch pieces.
3. Once the water is boiling, carefully place the apples in the steamer basket and cover with a fitted lid. Cook for 5 to 8 minutes, until the apples are fork-tender.
4. Carefully transfer the apples to a food processor. Purée until smooth, pausing to scrape down any larger chunks from the sides of the bowl.

Beef Purée

Here's protein, B vitamins, iron, and zinc. You can substitute lamb for beef in this purée. Choose a lean, sensitive cut like sirloin for poaching.
Cup water (or enough to cover the beef)

Prep time: 5 minutes | Cook time: : 10 minutes | Serves 5 (1-ounce) freezer cubes

- 8 ounces lean beef, cut into ½-inch cubes

1. In a small saucepan, bring the water to a simmer. Add the beef cubes.
2. Cover and simmer on medium heat until the beef is fully cooked and brown, about 10 minutes.
3. Remove the beef from the water and allow it to cool slightly, reserving the cooking liquid. Purée in a blender or food processor, adding a little of the poaching water for your desired consistency.

Carrot Purée

Carrots combine well with numerous spices, so they're perfect for experimentation. Serve with nutmeg, cinnamon, dill, thyme, parsley, rosemary, sage, or ginger.

Prep time: 5 minutes | Cook time: 5 minutes | Serves 10 (¼-CUP)

- 1 pound (about 5 medium) carrots

1. Rinse the carrots under running water and pat dry. Cut off both ends of the carrots and discard. Peel the carrots, then cut them into 1-inch pieces.
2. In a medium saucepan over medium heat, bring ½ cup of water to a boil. Put the carrots in the water and cook until fork-tender, about 5 minutes.
3. Remove the carrots, reserving the cooking water, and allow the carrots to cool slightly. Carefully transfer the carrots and cooking water to a food processor. Purée until smooth, pausing to scrape down any larger chunks from the sides of the bowl.

Parsnip Purée

This Purée isn't baby food. This sweet, nutty-tasting root vegetable resembles a white carrot. You'll need a lot of water to thin down Puréed parsnips.

Prep time: 5 minutes | Cook time: 10 minutes | Serves 6 (¼-CUP)

- ½ pound (about 3 medium) parsnips

1. Rinse the parsnips under running water and pat dry. Cut off both ends and discard. Peel the parsnips, then cut them into 1-inch pieces.
2. In a medium saucepan over medium heat, bring 1 cup of water to a boil. Add the parsnips to the water and cook until fork-tender, about 5 minutes.
3. Remove the parsnips, reserving the cooking water, and allow the parsnips to cool. Carefully transfer the parsnips and cooking water to a food processor. Purée until smooth, pausing to scrape down any larger chunks from the sides of the bowl and adding water as needed.

Roasted Beet Purée

Bib up! Beets are dirty yet abundant in vitamins A and C, zinc, copper, and iron. I prefer golden beets because their juice stains. If not, have wipes on hand. Roasting beets brings forth their natural sweetness.

Prep time: 5 minutes| Cook time: 50 minutes| Serves 6 (¼-CUP)

- 1 pound fresh beets

1. Preheat the oven to 375°F.
2. Rinse the beets well under running water, then slice off the greens.
3. Wrap the beets in aluminum foil with the edges sealed tightly at the top. Place the foil packet on a baking sheet and roast for 40 to 45 minutes or until the beets are fork-tender. Carefully open the foil (watch for the hot steam!) to let the beets cool.
4. Use tongs to transfer the beets to a resealable plastic bag. Then seal the bag and rub the outside of the bag to remove the beet skin. (This will prevent stains on your hands.)
5. Chop the beets into quarters, then Purée in a food processor until smooth, pausing to scrape down any larger chunks from the sides of the bowl and adding water by the tablespoon if needed.

Butternut Squash Purée

Butternut squash supports baby's growth and development. It's high in vitamins A and C, magnesium for strong bones, and potassium. Both recipes bake at the same temperature, so they go well together. Using a big squash, create Butternut Squash Mac 'n' Cheese.

Prep time: 5 minutes | Cook time: 45 minutes|Makes 16 (1-ounce) freezer cubes | Serving size: 2 tablespoons (1 cube)

- 1 medium butternut squash (about 2 pounds)
- ½ cup water

1. Preheat the oven to 425°F. Line a rimmed baking sheet with parchment paper.
2. Remove the ends and cut the butternut squash in half lengthwise. Scoop out and discard the seeds.
3. Place the squash, cut-side down, on the baking sheet. Bake for 30 to 45 minutes, or until soft. Remove from the oven and let it cool.
4. When cool enough to handle, use a spoon to scoop the cooked squash flesh out from the peel, and transfer to a blender or food processor. Blend until smooth, adding ½ cup of water (plus more as needed) to achieve the desired consistency.
5. Cool and serve, or transfer to an ice cube tray and freeze.

Homemade Baby Oatmeal

Homemade baby oatmeal is easier and cheaper than store-bought ones. For this recipe, use old-fashioned oats, not quick-cooking. Add cinnamon or apple or sweet potato Purée to oatmeal for taste.

Prep time: 5 minutes| Cook time: 5 minutes| Serves 3 (¼-CUP)

- ½ cup gluten-free old-fashioned rolled oats

1. Put the oats in a food processor and pulse for about 30 seconds, until the oats resemble a fine powder or flour.
2. In a small saucepan over medium heat, bring ½ cup of water to a boil. Add 2 tablespoons of ground oats, reduce the heat to low, and whisk for 3 to 5 minutes or until the mixture is thick. Cool slightly before serving. Add breast milk or formula to thin the mixture if desired.

Cauliflower Purée

Cauliflower may appear monotonous, but it's nutrient-dense. Fiber, vitamin B6, vitamin C, and antioxidants keep cells healthy. Purple, yellow, and green cauliflower are delicious and nutritious. Let your baby discover raw cauliflower's rough texture and brilliant hues.

Prep time: 5 minutes | Cook time: 10 minutes|Makes 16 (1-ounce) freezer cubes | Serving size: 2 tablespoons (1 cube)

- 1 medium head fresh cauliflower, cored and coarsely chopped (about 1½ pounds)
- ½ cup water

1. In a medium saucepan with a steamer basket or insert, bring about 1 inch of water to a simmer. Add the cauliflower. Cover and simmer over low heat for 7 to 10 minutes, or until the cauliflower is soft.
2. Remove from the heat and transfer the cauliflower to a blender or food processor. Blend until smooth, adding ½ cup of water (plus more as needed) to achieve the desired consistency.
3. Cool and serve, or transfer to an ice cube tray and freeze.

Pumpkin Purée

Pumpkin is a fall/winter favorite. It's also great for babies because it's sweet and silky. The flavor is worth the prep labor (and time, if you roast it). Pumpkin is high in fiber, A, C, and E.

Prep time: 5 minutes | Cook time: : 10 minutes| Serves 15 (1-ounce) freezer cubes

- 1½ pounds pumpkin, peeled, seeded, pulp removed, and cut into 1-inch cubes (or 1 [16-ounce] package frozen pumpkin, thawed)
- ¼ cup water, plus more if needed

1. Pour about ½ inch of water into a medium pot and set a steamer basket inside it. Arrange the pumpkin evenly inside the basket. Bring the water to a simmer over medium heat and steam for 10 to 15 minutes, until the pumpkin is soft (cover the pot to speed up the cooking time).
2. Transfer the cooked pumpkin and steaming water to a blender.
3. Add a pinch of herb or spice (if using).
4. Blend until combined and very smooth. (Add more water as needed; start by adding a little bit at a time, since you can always add more.)
5. .Transfer the purée to ice cube trays and freeze.

Pea Purée

Delicious fresh peas. Spring is the only time they're available. Using frozen peas for this purée reduces prep time. Layla didn't like pea purée by itself because of its strong flavor, but she loved it with carrots or a sweeter purée. If you want summer flavor, add frozen sweet corn with the peas.

Prep time: 5 minutes | Cook time: : 10 minutes| Serves 15 (1-ounce) freezer cubes

- 1 (16-ounce) package frozen peas
- ¼ cup water, plus more if needed

1. Pour about ½ inch of water into a medium pot and set a steamer basket inside it. Arrange the peas evenly inside the basket. Bring the water to a simmer over medium heat and steam for 10 to 15 minutes until the peas are soft (cover the pot to speed up the cooking time).
2. Transfer the cooked peas and steaming water to a blender.
3. Add a pinch of herb or spice (if using).
4. Blend until combined and very smooth. (Add more water as needed; start by adding a little bit at a time, since you can always add more.)
5. Transfer the purée to ice cube trays and freeze.

Oatmeal Purée

It's easy and cheaper to prepare baby oatmeal at home than to buy it. Baby cereal is finely powdered grains you can make at yourself. Oatmeal is full of fiber, vitamins, and minerals and blends nicely with fruit and veggie purées.

Prep time: 5 minutes | Cook time: : 10 minutes| Serves 15 (1-ounce) freezer cubes

- ½ cup rolled oats
- 2 cups water

1. In a food processor or blender, grind the oats to a fine powder.
2. In a small pot, bring the water to a simmer. Add the ground oats. Cook on low heat until the oats are soft, about 10 minutes. (This can also be done in the microwave, on high for 2 to 3 minutes.)
3. Transfer to ice cube trays and freeze.

Lentil Purée

Babies adore lentils' mild flavor. Mix this purée with a fruit or vegetable purée for added nutrition. Lentils contain fiber, protein, folate, and iron.

Prep time: 5 minutes | Cook time: : 60 minutes| Serves 15 (1-ounce) freezer cubes

- 1 cup dried lentils (red, yellow, brown, or green)
- 2½ cups water, plus more if needed

1. Put the lentils and water in a large pot and bring to a boil.
2. Reduce to a simmer. Let cook for 1 hour or until the lentils are very soft.
3. Transfer the cooked lentils and remaining water to a blender.
4. Blend until combined and very smooth. (Add more water if all the water has been absorbed. Start by adding a little bit at a time, as you can always add more.)
5. Add a pinch of herb or spice (if using).
6. Transfer to ice cube trays and freeze.

Barley Purée

After oatmeal, you can introduce other grains. Barley is a high-fiber, manganese, selenium, and magnesium infant cereal.

Prep time: 5 minutes | Cook time: : 10 minutes| Serves 15 (1-ounce) freezer cubes

- ½ cup dried barley
- 2 cups water

1. In a food processor or blender, grind the barley to a fine powder.
2. In a small pot, bring the water to a simmer. Add the ground barley. Cook on low heat until the barley is soft, about 10 minutes. (This can also be done in the microwave, on high for 2 to 3 minutes.)
3. Transfer to ice cube trays and freeze.

Chickpea Purée

This is "baby hummus" Add garlic and lemon zest to mimic store-bought hummus. Chickpeas contain protein, zinc, folate, and iron.

Prep time: 5 minutes | Cook time: : 20 minutes| Serves 15 (1-ounce) freezer cubes

- 2 cups water (or enough to cover the chickpeas)
- 2 (15-ounce) cans chickpeas, rinsed and drained

1. In a pot of water, boil the chickpeas for about 20 minutes, until soft.
2. Transfer the chickpeas to a blender, add about ½ cup of the boiling water and a pinch of herb or spice (if using), and purée.
3. Transfer to ice cube trays and freeze.

White Bean Purée

White beans are gentle and absorb flavors well. This purée adds protein to any purées you give your baby everyday. This recipe can use any bean. Bean options include black, pinto, kidney, and navy. If you can't soak dried beans overnight, canned beans reduce cooking time.

Prep time: 5 minutes, plus 8 hours to soak | Cook time: : 2 hours | Serves 15 (1-ounce) freezer cubes

- 2 cups water (or enough to cover the beans)
- 1 cup dried white beans, soaked overnight, rinsed and drained

1. In a pot of water, bring the beans to a boil, then reduce the heat and simmer until soft (about 2 hours).
2. Transfer the beans to a blender, add about ½ cup of the simmering water and a pinch of herb or spice (if using), and purée.
3. Transfer to ice cube trays and freeze.

Tofu Purée

Tofu can be beaten into a no-cook purée like avocado. Tofu's mild flavor blends well with others. As your infant gets older, add it to baby "smoothies" and fruit-vegetable purée combos.

Prep time: 5 minutes | Cook time: : 5 minutes| Serves 15 (1-ounce) freezer cubes

- 1 (12- to 16-ounce) block silken tofu, drained

1. In a high-speed blender, blend the tofu until smooth.
2. Transfer to ice cube trays and freeze.

Fish Purée

Your child can get protein from fish. You can substitute cod with rainbow trout or haddock. Most fishmongers remove all the bones, but you should still pick through the fillet before steaming.

Prep time: 5 minutes | Cook time: : 10 minutes| Serves 4 (1-ounce) freezer cubes

- 1 cup water (or enough to cover the fish)
- 8 ounces cod or other fish, skin and bones removed, cut into 4 pieces

1. In a small saucepan, bring the water to a simmer. Add the cod.
2. Cover and simmer over medium heat until the fish is opaque, 5 to 10 minutes.
3. Remove the cod from the water and allow it to cool slightly, reserving the cooking liquid. Purée in a blender or food processor, adding some of the poaching water for your desired consistency and a pinch of herb or spice (if using).

Poultry Purée

You can use any type of poultry and either white or dark flesh. Thin the purée as you make it, then thin it further before serving your baby.

Prep time: 5 minutes | Cook time: : 10 minutes| Serves 5 (1-ounce) freezer cubes

- 1 cup water (or enough to cover the poultry)
- 8 ounces boneless, skinless chicken or turkey thigh or breast, cut into about 8 pieces

1. In a small saucepan, bring the water to a simmer. Add the chicken or turkey.
2. Cover and simmer over medium heat until the poultry is cooked and opaque, 5 to 10 minutes.
3. Remove the poultry from the water and allow it to cool slightly, reserving the cooking liquid. Purée in a blender or food processor, adding a little of the poaching water for your desired consistency.

Chapter 3
Smooth Combination Purées(6-8 Months)

- This stage often combines two or more ingredients, thus exposing the baby to different flavors. When the baby has successfully gone through stage one, having no allergic reactions, it's ready to handle the thicker food consistency in stage two. They are more experienced eaters by now and can move food from the front to the back of their mouths. You can introduce well-cooked foods such as mashed potatoes with butter if your baby has started chewing. You can try different food consistencies if your baby gets more experience. If the liquid is used to make the food to thin, try reducing the liquid and watch how they react to the changes. Homemade food is better as you can mix flavors, add spices to suit your baby and build on familiar flavors. Six to 8 ounces of breast milk or infant formula with two to four tablespoons of Purée is the best ratio for your baby. Some of the recommended foods include, but are not limited to, sweet potato and chicken, apple and berries, butternut squash and corn. Unlike stage one, the baby's nutritional needs increase, but the concept remains the same. These nutritional needs include:

- Iron and zinc
- Vitamin D
- Breast milk or infant formula is also the primary source of nutrients and should be provided on demand. You shouldn't force your baby to breastfeed.

Spiced Pear Purée

Add some spices to spice things up. By adding cinnamon or cloves, you're broadening your infant's exposure, which is vital when feeding your newborn. Every step forward counts.

Prep time: 5 minutes | Cook time: 5 minutes | Makes 12 (1-ounce) freezer cubes | Serving size: 2 to 4 tablespoons (1 or 2 cubes)

- 5 small ripe pears, peeled
- Pinch ground cinnamon
- Pinch ground cloves

1. Slice the pears into quarters, removing and discarding the seeds and cores.
2. Transfer the pears to a blender and add the cinnamon and cloves. Blend until smooth, adding a splash of water, if needed.
3. Serve immediately, refrigerate in a sealed container for up to 3 days, or transfer to an ice cube tray and freeze for up to 3 months.

Pear Purée

This Pear Purée is like Applesauce, but more complex. Vanilla adds sweetness and warmth. I recommend ripe Anjou, Bartlett, or Comice pears. Most pears at the supermarket are hard, so ripen them on your counter until the narrow section gives when you press on it.

Prep time: 5 minutes | Cook time: 5 minutes | Makes 16 (1-ounce) freezer cubes | Serving size: 2 tablespoons (1 cube)

- 4 medium pears, cored, peeled, and coarsely chopped (about 1½ pounds)
- ¼ teaspoon vanilla extract (optional)

1. In a medium saucepan with a steamer basket or insert, bring about 1 inch of water to a simmer. Add the pears. Cover and simmer over low heat for 3 to 5 minutes, until the pears are soft.
2. Remove from the heat and transfer the pears to a blender or food processor. Add the vanilla (if using). Blend until smooth, adding a few tablespoons of water as needed to achieve the desired consistency.
3. Cool and serve, or transfer to an ice cube tray and freeze.

Very Berry Smoothie

Berries' sweet-tart flavor and fascinating texture will delight your infant. Use any berry mix you like. Serve this smoothie with Multigrain Cereal, Tropical Chia Seed Pudding, or plain whole-milk yogurt. Because it's thicker than water, your infant can practice sipping it from an open cup.

Prep time: 5 minutes | Makes 32 (1-ounce) freezer cubes | Serving size: ¼ cup (2 cubes)

- 6 cups fresh or frozen mixed berries (blueberries, raspberries, strawberries, blackberries)
- 1 cup water

1. Add the berries and water to a blender or food processor. Blend until mostly smooth, adding a few tablespoons of water as needed to achieve the desired consistency.
2. Serve, or transfer to an ice cube tray and freeze.

Cherry Almond Smoothie

Almonds provide protein for your kid. Delaying the introduction of tree nuts won't avoid an allergy. Smooth nut butters, like almond butter, are a safe method to offer your newborn tree nuts. Serve with whole-milk yogurt or cereal.

Prep time: 5 minutes | Makes 32 (1-ounce) freezer cubes | Serving size: ¼ cup (2 cubes)

- 4 cups fresh or frozen sweet cherries, pitted (about 1½ pounds)
- 1 cup creamy, unsalted almond butter
- 1 cup water

1. Add the cherries, almond butter, and water to a blender or food processor. Blend until mostly smooth, adding a few tablespoons of water as needed to achieve the desired consistency.
2. Serve, or transfer to an ice cube tray and freeze.

Chunky Carrots and Broccoli with Ginger

You may feed your kid stir-fry flavors in a texture that's suitable for them. Your infant will be attracted by the broccoli's rough florets while you cook. Add garlic or sesame oil for taste. Even low-sodium soy sauce is too salty for infants.

Prep time: 10 minutes | Cook time: 15 minutes|Makes 32 (1-ounce) freezer cubes | Serving size: ¼ cup (2 cubes)

- 5 medium carrots, peeled and coarsely chopped (about 1 pound)
- 1 medium head broccoli, coarsely chopped (about 1 pound)
- 1 tablespoon ginger, peeled and finely chopped
- 1 cup water

1. In a medium saucepan with a steamer basket or insert, bring about 1 inch of water to a simmer. Add the carrots and broccoli. Cover and simmer over low heat for 10 to 15 minutes, or until the carrots and broccoli are soft.
2. Remove from the heat and transfer the carrots and broccoli to a blender or food processor. Add the ginger. Blend until mostly smooth, adding 1 cup of water (plus more as needed) to achieve the desired consistency.
3. Cool and serve, or transfer to an ice cube tray and freeze.

Mashed Kiwi and Banana

Bananas and kiwis are a sweet-and-sour combo that babies love. One kiwi provides 100% of your baby's daily vitamin C needs. Choose somewhat yielding kiwis. Steam kiwis until they're soft enough to mash.

Prep time: 5 minutes|Makes 32 (1-ounce) freezer cubes | Serving size: ¼ cup (2 cubes)

- 6 kiwis, halved and flesh removed with a spoon
- 3 bananas

1. Combine the kiwis and bananas in a medium bowl. Mash with a fork until mostly smooth.
2. Serve, or transfer to an ice cube tray and freeze.

Mashed Sweet Potatoes and Banana

I first tried this meal 10 years ago at a Jersey Shore restaurant and thought it was a winner. Sweet potatoes' earthiness complements bananas' tropical fruitiness. Serve with baked apples and pears, creamed spinach, and lemon-parsley salmon.

Prep time: 5 minutes | Cook time: 45 minutes|Makes 32 (1-ounce) freezer cubes | Serving size: ¼ cup (2 cubes)

- 2 medium sweet potatoes (about 1 pound)
- 4 bananas
- ½ teaspoon ground cinnamon

1. Preheat the oven to 425°F. Line a rimmed baking sheet with aluminum foil or parchment paper.
2. Prick the sweet potatoes all over with a fork. Place the sweet potatoes on the prepared baking sheet and bake for about 45 minutes, or until soft.
3. Remove from the oven and let cool slightly. Use a spoon to scoop the cooked sweet potato flesh into a medium bowl. Add the bananas and cinnamon. Use a fork or potato masher to mash the sweet potato and banana until mostly smooth.
4. Serve, or transfer to an ice cube tray and freeze.

Mashed Roasted Zucchini with Thyme

Roasted zucchini is delicious. Roasting mild summer squash accentuates its inherent sweetness and creates a contrast between the soft inside and crisp outside. You can use zucchini, yellow squash, pattypan squash, or tatuma squash. Zucchini skin is edible, but I recommend scoring it before roasting to make it more baby-friendly.

Prep time: 10 minutes | Cook time: 20 minutes|Makes 32 (1-ounce) freezer cubes | Serving size: ¼ cup (2 cubes)

- 5 medium zucchini (about 1½ pounds)
- 1 tablespoon olive oil
- 1 teaspoon dried thyme

1. Preheat the oven to 425°F. Line a rimmed baking sheet with parchment paper.
2. Use a fork to gently score all over the outer peel of the zucchini. Then cut into ½-inch rounds.
3. Transfer the zucchini rounds to the prepared baking sheet. Add the olive oil and thyme and toss to coat. Arrange the zucchini rounds in a single layer.
4. Bake for 20 minutes, flipping halfway during cooking, or until the zucchini is soft and lightly browned.
5. Remove from the oven and let cool slightly. Use a fork to mash the zucchini until mostly smooth, removing any large pieces of peel.
6. Serve, or transfer to an ice cube tray and freeze.

Chunky Green Beans with Lemon

When my daughter was a baby, I attempted puréeing green beans but realized they shouldn't be smooth. This recipe uses lemon juice and zest to enhance the flavor of chunky green beans. Green beans go well with mashed potatoes with bell pepper and sardines, chicken and sweet potato stew, or scrambled eggs.

Prep time: 5 minutes | Cook time: 15 minutes|Makes 32 (1-ounce) freezer cubes | Serving size: ¼ cup (2 cubes)

- 2 pounds green beans, trimmed
- Juice of ½ lemon (about 1 tablespoon)
- Zest of ½ lemon (about 1 teaspoon)
- ½ cup water

1. In a medium saucepan with a steamer basket or insert, bring about 1 inch of water to a simmer. Add the green beans. Cover and simmer over low heat for 10 to 15 minutes, or until the green beans are soft.
2. Remove from the heat and transfer the green beans to a blender or food processor. Add the lemon juice and lemon zest. Blend until mostly smooth, adding ½ cup of water (plus more as needed) to achieve the desired consistency.
3. Cool and serve, or transfer to an ice cube tray and freeze.

Avocado and Banana Purée

The combination of creamy avocado and sweet banana is one of Julian's favorites. As he develops, we prepare smoothies with it. This mix provides healthful fat, potassium, and vitamin C.

Prep time: 5 minutes | Cook time: 5 minutes| Serves 2 (2-OUNCE)

- 3 (1-ounce) freezer tray cubes avocado Purée, thawed
- 1 (1-ounce) freezer tray cube banana purée, thawed
- Pinch ground cloves, nutmeg, ginger, or cinnamon
-

1. Combine the thawed Purées in a small bowl. Add one of the recommended spices. Mix well with a spoon. If needed, thin the Purée with breast milk, formula, or water to achieve the desired consistency.
2. Store any unoffered Purée in the refrigerator for up to 2 days. Do not refreeze.

Mashed Eggplant with Garlic

This recipe is inspired by the Middle Eastern dip baba ghanoush. When the flesh is mushy and the skin darkens and collapses, it's done. Roasted garlic gives a toasted taste to the creamy eggplant in this recipe.

Prep time: 10 minutes | Cook time: 40 minutes|Makes 32 (1-ounce) freezer cubes | Serving size: ¼ cup (2 cubes)

- 2 medium eggplants (about 2 to 3 pounds)
- 1 tablespoon plus 2 teaspoons olive oil, divided
- 4 garlic cloves, peeled and left whole

1. Preheat the oven to 425°F. Line a rimmed baking sheet with parchment paper.
2. Cut the eggplant in half lengthwise. Rub the eggplant halves with 1 tablespoon of olive oil, and place cut-side down on the prepared baking sheet. Bake for 30 to 40 minutes, or until the eggplant is very soft. Remove from the oven and let cool slightly.
3. While the eggplant is cooking, place the garlic cloves and 2 teaspoons of olive oil on a small square of aluminum foil. Fold the aluminum foil around the garlic to create a sealed packet. Bake for 20 to 30 minutes, or until the garlic is soft.
4. Remove from the oven and let cool slightly. Use a spoon to scoop the eggplant flesh out of the skin into a medium bowl. Add the garlic and mash with a fork until mostly smooth.
5. Serve, or transfer to an ice cube tray and freeze.

Sweet Potato and Spinach Purée

Sweet potatoes (or yams) and spinach are both superfoods, so combine them in this Purée. Iron, calcium, vitamins, and antioxidants are abundant.

Prep time: 5 minutes | Cook time: 5 minutes| Serves 2 (2-OUNCE)

- 3 (1-ounce) freezer tray cubes sweet potato purée, thawed
- 1 (1-ounce) freezer tray cube spinach purée, thawed
- Pinch ground cloves

1. Combine the thawed Purées in a small bowl. Add the cloves. Mix well with a spoon. If needed, thin the Purée with breast milk, formula, or water to achieve the desired consistency.
2. Spoon the portion you plan to serve to your baby into a small pot. Return the rest of the Purée to the refrigerator, where it can be stored for up to 3 days. Do not refreeze.
3. Gently warm the Purée on the stove top over low heat before serving. Discard any uneaten Purée.

Pumpkin and Apple Purée

This fall Purée is perfect with pumpkins and apples. You can use canned organic pumpkin if you don't have pumpkin Purée in your freezer or don't want to prepare it from scratch. Check the label for additions.

Prep time: 5 minutes | Cook time: 5 minutes| Serves 2 (2-OUNCE)

- 2 (1-ounce) freezer tray cubes pumpkin purée, thawed
- 2 (1-ounce) freezer tray cubes apple purée, thawed
- Pinch ground cloves

1. Combine the thawed Purées in a small bowl. Add the cloves. Mix well with a spoon. If needed, thin the Purée with breast milk, formula, or water to achieve the desired consistency.
2. Spoon the portion you plan to serve to your baby into a small pot. Return the rest of the Purée to the refrigerator, where it can be stored for up to 3 days. Do not refreeze.
3. Gently warm the Purée on the stove top over low heat before serving. Discard any uneaten Purée.

Asparagus and Tofu Purée

This protein-rich Purée supports growth. Mild tofu allows the asparagus to shine. Make your Purée with asparagus in March and April, or buy it frozen for year-round flavor.

Prep time: 5 minutes | Cook time: 5 minutes| Serves 2 (2-OUNCE)

- 2 (1-ounce) freezer tray cubes asparagus purée, thawed
- 2 (1-ounce) freezer tray cubes tofu purée, thawed
- Pinch ground coriander or cumin

1. Combine the thawed Purées in a small bowl. Add the coriander or cumin. Mix well with a spoon. If needed, thin the Purée with breast milk, formula, or water to achieve the desired consistency.
2. Spoon the portion you plan to serve to your baby into a small pot. Return the rest of the Purée to the refrigerator, where it can be stored for up to 3 days. Do not refreeze.
3. Gently warm the Purée on the stove top over low heat before serving. Discard any uneaten Purée.

Green Bean and Sweet Potato Purée

You can introduce your kid to Thanksgiving delicacies before November. This dish is delicious year-round.

Prep time: 5 minutes | Cook time: 5 minutes| Serves 2 (2-OUNCE)

- 2 (1-ounce) freezer tray cubes green bean purée, thawed
- 2 (1-ounce) freezer tray cubes sweet potato purée, thawed

1. Combine the thawed Purées in a small bowl. Mix well with a spoon. If needed, thin the Purée with breast milk, formula, or water to achieve the desired consistency.
2. Spoon the portion you plan to serve to your baby into a small pot. Return the rest of the Purée to the refrigerator, where it can be stored for up to 3 days. Do not refreeze.
3. Gently warm the Purée on the stove top over low heat before serving. Discard any uneaten Purée.

Black Bean and Mango Purée

Never before has protein tasted quite so satisfying. This combination Purée has a sweet flavor that is pleasing to the palate and a smooth consistency thanks to the mango, which provides a contrast to the bean's starchiness.

Prep time: 5 minutes | Cook time: 5 minutes| Serves 2 (2-OUNCE)

- 3 (1-ounce) freezer tray cubes black bean purée, thawed
- 1 (1-ounce) freezer tray cube mango purée, thawed
- Pinch ground cumin

1. Combine the thawed Purées in a small bowl. Add the cumin. Mix well with a spoon. If needed, thin the Purée with breast milk, formula, or water to achieve the desired consistency.
2. Spoon the portion you plan to serve to your baby into a small pot. Return the rest of the Purée to the refrigerator, where it can be stored for up to 3 days. Do not refreeze.
3. Gently warm the Purée on the stove top over low heat before serving. Discard any uneaten Purée.

Broccoli and Pear Purée

This mix of pear and broccoli will keep your baby's mouth open. Both components are fiber-rich, so they're beneficial for constipated babies.

Prep time: 5 minutes | Cook time: 5 minutes| Serves 2 (2-OUNCE)

- 2 (1-ounce) freezer tray cubes broccoli purée, thawed
- 2 (1-ounce) freezer tray cubes pear purée, thawed

1. Combine the thawed Purées in a small bowl. Mix well with a spoon. If needed, thin the Purée with breast milk, formula, or water to achieve the desired consistency.
2. Spoon the portion you plan to serve to your baby into a small pot. Return the rest of the Purée to the refrigerator, where it can be stored for up to 3 days. Do not refreeze.
3. Gently warm the Purée on the stove top over low heat before serving. Discard any uneaten Purée.

Blueberry and Yogurt Purée

This creamy, zesty purée is baby-approved. Blueberries provide antioxidants and flavor to this purée. The yogurt contains probiotics and calcium to promote your baby's digestive and bone health.

Prep time: 5 minutes | Cook time: 5 minutes|Serves 2 (2-OUNCE)

- 1 (1-ounce) freezer tray cube blueberry purée, thawed
- 3 ounces plain full-fat yogurt

1. Combine the thawed Purée and the yogurt in a small bowl. Mix well with a spoon. If needed, thin the Purée with breast milk, formula, or water to achieve the desired consistency.
2. Store any unoffered Purée in the refrigerator for up to 3 days. Do not refreeze.

Pea and Carrot Purée

This veggie pairing is a classic: High in protein, fiber, and vitamins A, B, and C for muscular growth and digestion.

Prep time: 5 minutes | Cook time: 5 minutes|Serves 2 (2-OUNCE)

- 2 (1-ounce) freezer tray cubes pea purée, thawed
- 2 (1-ounce) freezer tray cubes carrot purée, thawed

1. Combine the thawed Purées in a small bowl. Mix well with a spoon. If needed, thin the Purée with breast milk, formula, or water to achieve the desired consistency.
2. Spoon the portion you plan to serve to your baby into a small pot. Return the rest of the Purée to the refrigerator, where it can be stored for up to 3 days. Do not refreeze.
3. Gently warm the Purée on the stove top over low heat before serving. Discard any uneaten Purée.

Butternut Squash and Swiss Chard Purée

When butternut squash is in season, chard is plentiful. This mild, sweet purée is a wonderful early pairing. As your baby develops, sauté chard in olive oil and roast squash before Puréeing to enhance their aromas.

Prep time: 5 minutes | Cook time: 5 minutes|Serves 2 (2-OUNCE)

- 3 (1-ounce) freezer tray cubes butternut squash purée, thawed
- 1 (1-ounce) freezer tray cube Swiss chard purée, thawed
- Pinch ground nutmeg

1. Combine the thawed Purées in a small bowl. Add the nutmeg. Mix well with a spoon. If needed, thin the Purée with breast milk, formula, or water to achieve the desired consistency.
2. Spoon the portion you plan to serve to your baby into a small pot. Return the rest of the Purée to the refrigerator, where it can be stored for up to 3 days. Do not refreeze.
3. Gently warm the Purée on the stove top over low heat before serving. Discard any uneaten Purée.

Edamame and Apricot Purée

Edamame are high in protein and fiber, and apricots add antioxidants and sweetness.

Prep time: 5 minutes | Cook time: 5 minutes|Serves 2 (2-OUNCE)

3 (1-ounce) freezer tray cubes edamame purée, thawed
1 (1-ounce) freezer tray cube apricot purée, thawed
Pinch ground allspice

1. Combine the thawed Purées in a small bowl. Add the allspice. Mix well with a spoon. If needed, thin the Purée with breast milk, formula, or water to achieve the desired consistency.
2. Store any unoffered Purée in the refrigerator for up to 3 days. Do not refreeze.

Zucchini and Brown Rice Cereal Purée

If you want to ease your baby's pallet into combinations, try this Purée (without the oregano). Oregano gives it a kick to introduce your kid to Mediterranean flavor.

Prep time: 5 minutes | Cook time: 5 minutes|Serves 2 (2-ounce)

- 2 (1-ounce) freezer tray cubes zucchini purée, thawed
- 2 (1-ounce) freezer tray cubes brown rice cereal, thawed
- ⅛ teaspoon dried oregano

1. Combine the thawed Purées in a small bowl. Add the oregano. Mix well with a spoon. If needed, thin the Purée with breast milk, formula, or water to achieve the desired consistency.
2. Spoon the portion you plan to serve to your baby into a small pot. Return the rest of the Purée to the refrigerator, where it can be stored for up to 3 days. Do not refreeze.
3. Gently warm the Purée on the stove top over low heat before serving. Discard any uneaten Purée.

Broccoli and Pinto Bean Purée

Broccoli alone can be light, so adding pinto beans makes it more filling and protein-rich.

Prep time: 5 minutes | Cook time: 5 minutes|Serves 1 (5-ounce)

- 3 (1-ounce) freezer tray cubes broccoli purée, thawed
- 2 (1-ounce) freezer tray cubes pinto bean purée, thawed
- Pinch garlic powder

1. Combine the thawed Purées in a small bowl. Add the garlic powder. Mix well with a spoon. If needed, thin the Purée with breast milk, formula, or water to achieve the desired consistency.
2. Spoon the portion you plan to serve to your baby into a small pot. Return the rest of the Purée to the refrigerator, where it can be stored for up to 3 days. Do not refreeze.
3. Gently warm the Purée on the stove top over low heat before serving. Discard any uneaten Purée.3

Chickpea and Mango Purée

Chickpeas with mango combine sweet and earthy flavors. Chickpeas are fiber-rich, so this purée is helpful if previous solid foods have caused constipation.

Prep time: 5 minutes | Cook time: 5 minutes|Serves 2 (2-ounce)

- 3 (1-ounce) freezer tray cubes chickpea purée, thawed
- 1 (1-ounce) freezer tray cube mango purée, thawed
- Pinch ground ginger

1. Combine the thawed Purées in a small bowl. Add the ginger. Mix well with a spoon. If needed, thin the Purée with breast milk, formula, or water to achieve the desired consistency.
2. Store any unoffered Purée in the refrigerator for up to 3 days. Do not refreeze.

Kale and Banana Purée

This kale and banana purée is filled with antioxidants that boost baby's growth, health, and immunity. Vitamin A-rich Purée helps baby's eyesight.

Prep time: 5 minutes | Cook time: 5 minutes|Serves 2 (2-ounce)

- 2 (1-ounce) freezer tray cubes kale purée, thawed
- 2 (1-ounce) freezer tray cubes banana purée, thawed
- Pinch ground nutmeg

1. Combine the thawed Purées in a small bowl. Add the nutmeg. Mix well with a spoon. If needed, thin the Purée with breast milk, formula, or water to achieve the desired consistency.
2. Store any unoffered Purée in the refrigerator for up to 2 days. Do not refreeze.

Oat and Pear Purée

Pears give oat cereal a subtle sweetness. Pears provide fiber to keep your infant regular.

Prep time: 5 minutes | Cook time: 5 minutes|Serves 2 (2-ounce)

- Pears add a wonderfully mild sweetness to the blank slate of oat cereal. To boot, pears are a great source of fiber to keep your baby regular.
- 3 (1-ounce) freezer tray cubes oat cereal, thawed
- 1 (1-ounce) freezer tray cube pear purée, thawed

1. Combine the thawed Purées in a small bowl. Mix well with a spoon. If needed, thin the Purée with breast milk, formula, or water to achieve the desired consistency.
2. Store any unoffered Purée in the refrigerator for up to 3 days. Do not refreeze.

Cauliflower and Broccoli Purée

This purée is a convenient way to feed your baby nutritious vegetables that are high in fiber and provide essential nutrients for developing bodies.

Prep time: 5 minutes | Cook time: 5 minutes| Serves 3 (1-ounce)

- 2 (1-ounce) freezer tray cubes cauliflower purée, thawed
- 1 (1-ounce) freezer tray cube broccoli purée, thawed

1. Combine the thawed Purées in a small bowl. Mix well with a spoon. If needed, thin the Purée with breast milk, formula, or water to achieve the desired consistency.
2. Spoon the portion you plan to serve to your baby into a small pot. Return the rest of the Purée to the refrigerator, where it can be stored for up to 3 days. Do not refreeze.
3. Gently warm the Purée on the stove top over low heat before serving. Discard any uneaten Purée.

Banana-Avocado Purée

Bananas and avocados don't need to be cooked to be digestible by babies. Mash and serve these fruits. Dirt and bacteria from the peel might penetrate the fruit as it's cut.

Prep time: 5 minutes| Cook time: 10 minutes| Serves 3 (¼-CUP)

- ½ ripe medium avocado
- ½ banana

1. Rinse the avocado under running water and pat dry. Using a large chef's knife, cut the avocado in half lengthwise, turning the fruit as your knife hits the pit. Do this very carefully to avoid cutting your hand. Twist and pull to create two halves.
2. To remove the pit, hold the pitted half in a kitchen towel, then carefully tap the middle of the knife into the pit. Twist the knife to remove the pit. Use a spoon to scoop out the flesh.
3. In a small bowl, combine the banana and avocado. Mash with a fork or Purée in a blender or food processor until smooth. Serve immediately.

Broccoli-Cauliflower Purée

All four of my kids eat broccoli and cauliflower mash as infants, and I believe it's why. Cauliflower steams longer than broccoli, so I put it on the bottom. Rinsing cooked vegetables in cold water will keep the broccoli color bright and fresh.

Prep time: 5 minutes| Cook time: 10 minutes| Serves 8 (¼-CUP)

- 1½ cups fresh broccoli florets
- 1½ cups fresh cauliflower florets

1. Fill a saucepan halfway with water. Set a steamer basket in the pan and place the pan over medium heat.
2. Once the water is boiling, carefully place the cauliflower in the steamer basket and the broccoli on top. Cover with a fitted lid. Cook for 7 to 9 minutes until fork-tender.
3. Using oven mitts, remove the steamer basket from the stove, and rinse the vegetables under cold running water for at least 10 seconds.
4. Carefully transfer the vegetables to a food processor. Purée until smooth, pausing to scrape down any larger chunks from the sides of the bowl. If the mixture is too thick, add the water you used to steam the vegetables, 1 tablespoon at a time, to achieve the desired consistency.

Spinach-Pear Purée

Peeling pears before heating and Puréeing eases baby's digestion. After a month of eating pears, you can leave the skin on. Same guideline for fruits with skins you consume.

Prep time: 5 minutes| Cook time: 10 minutes| Serves 6 (¼-CUP)

- 1 pound (3 or 4 medium) pears
- 1½ cups packed baby spinach

1. Rinse the pears under running water and pat them dry with a paper towel.
2. Fill a saucepan halfway with water. Top it with a steamer basket and place it over medium heat.
3. Peel and core the pears. Cut them into 1-inch pieces.
4. When the water is boiling, carefully place the pears in the steamer basket. Place the spinach on top of the pears and cover with a fitted lid. Cook for 5 to 8 minutes until the pears are fork-tender and the spinach is wilted.
5. Using oven mitts and a rubber spatula, transfer the ingredients to a food processor. Purée until smooth, pausing to scrape down any larger chunks from the sides of the bowl.

Fruit And Veggie Yogurt Purée

When my oldest started solids, the sugar concentration of baby yogurt shocked me. Even organic baby yogurts have extra sugar. Plain whole-milk yogurt with natural sweetener is helpful for babies' brain development.

Prep time: 5 minutes| Cook time: 5 minutes| Serves 2 (¼-CUP)

- ½ cup plain whole-milk yogurt
- 1 ounce butternut squash purée
- 1 ounce apple purée

1. In a medium bowl, stir together the yogurt, squash Purée, and apple Purée and serve immediately.
2. Leftover frozen Purées are your best friend for this recipe. Ice cube tray servings are often 1 ounce in size, so pop out two Purée cubes from your freezer stash to make this recipe in a pinch.

Multigrain Porridge

Why buy boring baby cereal when you can create your own? Protein, fiber, and minerals produce a nutritious, tasty baby cereal. You should eat some before blending the remainder for your kid.

Prep time: 5 minutes| Cook time: 30 minutes| Serves 12 (¼-CUP)

- ¼ cup wheat berries
- ¼ cup farro
- ¼ cup pearled barley

1. In a fine-mesh strainer, rinse the wheat berries, farro, and barley under cool running water.
2. Put the grains in a medium saucepan, then toast them over medium heat for about 2 minutes, stirring occasionally.
3. Carefully add 3 cups of water to the saucepan. (It will sizzle.) Bring the water to a boil, then reduce the heat to low and cook until the grains are soft and chewy, about 30 minutes. Drain any excess water through a fine-mesh strainer.
4. Transfer the grains to a food processor and Purée until mostly smooth, about 1 minute, adding water if necessary to reach your desired consistency.

Breakfast Cereal with Brown Rice And Quinoa

Too much quinoa can be difficult for beginning eaters to stomach, so I blend it with brown rice for a gluten-free breakfast cereal.

PREP TIME: 5 MINUTES| COOK TIME: 50 MINUTES| SERVES 6 (¼-CUP)

- ¼ cup brown rice
- ¼ cup quinoa
- 1½ cups water

1. In a fine-mesh strainer, rinse the rice and quinoa under cool running water.
2. In a medium saucepan, combine the water, rice, and quinoa. Bring to a boil over medium-high heat, then reduce the heat to low, cover the pan, and simmer for 40 minutes or until the rice and quinoa are tender.
3. Transfer the mixture to a food processor. Purée until the mixture is smooth, adding water as needed to reach your desired consistency.

Chapter 4
Chunky Combination Purées(9-12 Months)

- Chunky Purées are for older babies with better chewing skills. The Purée at this stage is a chunker texture as your baby is exploring more food options. The baby can eat the same meal as the rest of the family if served properly. Any food should be cut into small bits to make it easier to hold. You may decide to give your baby a bigger piece of soft food, such as a banana so it can self-feed. Be careful not to give your baby a piece of raw food that they could choke on. Something like raw carrot and whole grapes is not recommended. In stages one and two, breast milk or infant formula is the primary source of nutrients. The baby will most likely take six to eight ounces of milk three to four times a day. Your baby will require foods rich in vitamin D, zinc and iron. The number of nutrients your baby needs will depend on the type of foods you feed it. If you are concerned, consult a pediatrician.

Cottage Cheese with Mix-Ins

Cottage cheese comes in varied textures: small curd, large curd, and mixed. Choose one with whole milk and no extra salt. Whole-milk dairy is best for your baby's growing brain for the first two years. If the infant doesn't like it, try it again with a different add-in or texture.

Prep time: 5 minutes | Cook time: 5 minutes | Serves 1

- ⅓ cup cottage cheese (no salt added)
- Soft fruit, such as berries, pears, or peeled stone fruits

1. Add the cottage cheese to your baby's bowl.
2. In a separate small bowl, mash the fruit with a fork.
3. Add the mashed fruit to cottage cheese—you may stir, blend, or leave it on top for different experiences.

Sweet Potato, Apple, and Lentil Purée

Purées often neglect lentils. They provide protein, vitamins, antioxidants, fiber, and iron. Lentils mix and cook effortlessly.

Prep time: 5 minutes | Cook time: 55 minutes | Serves

- 1 cup water or low-sodium chicken or vegetable broth
- ½ cup dry lentils, rinsed
- 1 sweet potato, peeled and cut into chunks
- 2 apples, peeled, cored, and cut into chunks
- ¼ teaspoon cinnamon

1. In a saucepan, bring the water to a boil and add the lentils.
2. Cover the pot and turn the heat down to let the lentils simmer for 30 to 40 minutes, until all the liquid is absorbed and the lentils are soft.
3. In another pot (or rice cooker), insert a steamer tray and add a little water.
4. Bring the water to a boil, then add the sweet potato and apples. Steam for 10 minutes, or until cooked through and soft.
5. Blend the lentils, sweet potato, apples, and cinnamon with a blender or food processor until smooth.

Apple and Raspberry Purée

Roasting fruits and vegetables brings forth a lovely caramel flavor. Roasted apples with mashed raspberry provide a vibrant baby food.

Prep time: 5 minutes | Cook time: 35 minutes | Serves 1

- 1 tablespoon olive oil or unsalted butter
- 1 apple, peeled, cored, and chopped into thumb-size chunks
- Pinch cinnamon (optional)
- ¼ cup raspberries

1. Preheat the oven to 350°F.
2. Prepare a baking sheet by lining it with foil and coating it lightly with the olive oil or butter.
3. Lay the apple chunks in a single layer on the prepared baking sheet. Lightly dust with cinnamon, if using.
4. Bake for 25 to 30 minutes, or until soft.
5. Soak the raspberries in a separate bowl of water for a few minutes, then drain.
6. Let the apples cool, then add them to the raspberries. Blend or mash together.

Beef and Pumpkin Purée

Pair meat purée with a creamy vegetable to counteract its dryness. This fall-friendly meal uses fresh pumpkin. Pumpkin is rich in bone-building vitamin K.

Prep time: 5 minutes | Cook time: 45 minutes | Serves 6

- 8 ounces chuck beef, trimmed and chopped
- 1 cup chopped pumpkin or 1 (15-ounce) can pumpkin purée
- 1 white or sweet potato, peeled and chopped
- 1 bay leaf

1. Put the beef, chopped pumpkin, potato, and bay leaf in a saucepan and cover with water. If using pumpkin purée, reserve it to add later.
2. Cover the pot and bring to a boil, then simmer for about 35 minutes. Add water as needed.
3. Remove the meat and vegetables from the pot but reserve the cooking liquid. Discard the bay leaf.
4. Blend all the ingredients together. (If you're using pumpkin purée, add it now.) Add some cooking liquid a little at a time until the desired texture is reached.

Chicken and Mango Purée

Mango's sweetness and creaminess complement chicken purée. This dish's sweet-and-savory combination will delight your kid. Mangos are abundant in vitamin C, vitamin A, and folate for growth and development. This recipe goes well with Brown Rice.

Prep time: 5 minutes | Cook time: 45 minutes| Serves 12

- 1 tablespoon olive oil
- 2 boneless, skinless chicken thighs
- 1 mango, peeled, pitted, and chopped
- 4 carrots, peeled and sliced
- 1 cup low-sodium chicken or vegetable broth

1. Preheat the oven to 350°F. Prepare a baking sheet by coating it lightly with the olive oil.
2. Place the chicken, mango, and carrots on the foil, then wrap them in the foil like a package, sealing all edges.
3. Bake for 30 to 45 minutes, until the internal temperature of the chicken reaches 165°F.
4. Let the foods cool slightly, then blend them, slowly adding the broth until the desired texture has been reached.

Spinach, Pumpkin, and Chickpeas

This recipe's pumpkin purée is delicately sweet. Combining it with protein-packed chickpeas and oats gives it a thick consistency as your baby eats more solid foods. Good for freezing.

Prep time: 5 minutes | Cook time: 15 minutes| Serves 6

½ cup water
¼ cup old-fashioned oats
1 cup canned chickpeas, drained and rinsed
1 cup spinach, stems trimmed
½ cup broccoli florets, steamed
8 ounces low-sodium vegetable broth
½ cup canned pumpkin
½ teaspoon coriander

1. In a saucepan, bring the water to a boil.
2. Add the oats to the water and simmer for 5 minutes over low heat.
3. Combine the chickpeas, spinach, broccoli, and vegetable broth in a blender. Pulse into small chunks.
4. Add the oats, pumpkin, and coriander to the blender mixture and pulse until just mixed.

Carrot, Sweet Potato, and Brown Rice

This dish is orange. Instead of puréeing carrots and sweet potatoes, pulse them to a chunky texture. Brown rice makes a smooth, adaptable purée.

Prep time: 5 minutes | Cook time: 15 minutes| Serves 6

- 1 sweet potato, peeled and diced
- 2 large carrots, peeled and diced
- ¾-inch piece fresh ginger, grated
- ½ cup brown rice

1. Boil the sweet potato and carrots for 7 to 10 minutes, or until fork-tender.
2. Allow the foods to cool to room temperature.
3. Pulse the sweet potato, carrots, ginger, and brown rice in a blender until the mixture is in small chunks.

Roasted Pumpkin and Coconut Rice

Roasting your own pumpkin adds taste. Coconut milk adds a creamy mouthfeel to sweet meals. Mango is tasty.

Prep time: 5 minutes | Cook time: 35 minutes| Serves 14

- 1 Amish Pie pumpkin
- 1 tablespoon olive oil
- ½-inch piece ginger, peeled
- 4 ounces coconut water
- 1½ cups mango chunks
- 4 ounces full-fat canned coconut milk
- ½ cup brown rice

1. Preheat the oven to 350°F.
2. Cut the pumpkin into quarters, removing the seeds and pith. Rub the olive oil on the skin.
3. Line a shallow baking dish with parchment paper. Place the pumpkin skin-side up in the dish and roast for 20 minutes. Allow to cool completely.
4. Gently peel away the pumpkin's skin and discard.
5. Place 1 cup of roasted pumpkin, ginger, coconut water, and mango in a blender and purée until smooth.
6. In a bowl, mix the purée and coconut milk. Add the brown rice, mixing well.
7. Mash with a fork for smaller bites and serve.

Strawberry, Beet, Purple Carrot, and Chia Seeds

Purple carrots are colorful and nutritious. They're sweeter than oranges, but either can be used. Beets add sweetness to this dish, while strawberries offer color and sharpness. Try several beet cultivars for flavor. This recipe's chia seeds aid constipated babies.

Prep time: 5 minutes | Cook time: 35 minutes| Serves 6

- 1 beet
- 2 purple carrots, peeled and quartered
- 1 kiwifruit, peeled, quartered, and white pith removed from center
- 4 ounces pear nectar
- 10 strawberries, hulled and cut into bite-size chunks
- 1 tablespoon chia seeds

1. Preheat the oven to 350°F.
2. Cut off the top of the beet, then cut the beet in half and poke each side with a fork.
3. Line a baking sheet with parchment paper. Place the beet on the prepared baking sheet and bake for 25 minutes, until fork-tender.
4. Let the beet cool to room temperature, then remove its tough outer skin. Cut into bite-size chunks.
5. Steam the carrots in a pot with shallow water until tender. Drain.
6. Put the kiwifruit, beet, purple carrots, pear nectar, and strawberries in a blender. Pulse until smooth.
7. Place the purée in a bowl, sprinkle with the chia seeds, and stir well to mix.
8. Cool to room temperature for 20 minutes before serving.

Tropical Fruits Mash-Up

This delectable recipe needs a hammock and coastal wind. Baby can start self-feeding with this purée's bite-size bits. If puréed, this recipe makes fantastic frozen pops. Freeze the purée for 4-6 hours or overnight.

Prep time: 5 minutes | Cook time: 5 minutes| Serves 6

- 1 banana (red, if available)
- 2 ounces guava nectar
- 4 ounces pineapple nectar
- 8 ounces cubed mango, diced
- 1 pear, peeled, cored, and diced
- 2 apples, peeled, cored, and diced

1. Place the banana, guava nectar, and pineapple nectar in a blender.
2. Purée until smooth.
3. Add the purée to the diced mango, pear, and apples and mix well.

Apple-Cinnamon Oatmeal Fingers

Filling oatmeal is flexible. Healthy Little Foodies' oatmeal fingers travel nicely and are loved by little ones. This gentle recipe will appeal more to babies than to adults, who lack subtle nuances.

Prep time: 5 minutes | Cook time: 5 minutes| Serves 6

4 tablespoons old-fashioned oats
2 tablespoons milk (milk alternative for vegan option)
2 tablespoons applesauce
1 tablespoon peeled and grated apple
½ teaspoon cinnamon

1. In a medium bowl, mix the oats, milk, and applesauce. Soak until the oats are mushy.
2. .Stir in the grated apple and cinnamon.
3. 3.Using the back of a spoon, press the mixture into a 9-by-13-inch baking dish.
4. 4.Microwave on high for 2 minutes.
5. 5.Cut into fingers while the food is hot, then let it cool to room temperature before serving.

Pear and Carrot Purée

This delightful, readily digested, and attractive Purée combines a gently sweet vegetable and fruit. It's rich in vitamins A and C, providing antioxidants for your infant.

Prep time: 5 minutes | Cook time: 10 minutes|Serves 2 (2-OUNCE)

- ½ pear, peeled, cored, and cut into ¼-inch dice
- 3 (1-ounce) freezer tray cubes carrot Purée, thawed
- ⅛ teaspoon dried thyme or ¼ teaspoon minced fresh thyme

1. In a medium saucepan with a steamer insert, bring about 1 inch of water to a simmer. Steam the pear, covered, until tender, about 6 minutes.
2. Add the pear, carrot Purée, and thyme to a sauté pan or small pot. Mix until combined and gently warm the Purée on the stove top over low heat before serving. Discard any uneaten Purée.

Lentil, Red Pepper, and Coconut Purée

Coconut milk and red bell peppers flavor these healthful lentils. This is a hearty last meal of the day.

Prep time: 5 minutes | Cook time: 10 minutes | Serves 8 (2-OUNCE)

- 1 cup cooked lentils, drained if canned
- 1 red bell pepper stemmed, seeded, and cut into ¼-inch dice
- ¼ cup coconut milk
- ¼ cup water
- ¼ teaspoon nutmeg

1. In a medium saucepan, bring the lentils, red pepper, coconut milk, water, and nutmeg to a simmer, stirring occasionally. Simmer until the red peppers are soft, about 6 minutes.
2. Transfer half of the mixture to a blender or food processor and Purée until smooth. If needed, thin the Purée with breast milk, formula, or water to achieve the desired consistency.
3. Stir the Puréed mixture back into the remaining unPuréed ingredient mixture. Cool slightly before serving. Store any unoffered Purée in the refrigerator for up to 3 days or in the freezer for up to 6 months.

White Bean and Leek Purée

If your child likes savory Purées, try this one. Julian adored this Purée, and we prepared it so often. If you don't have a leek, use 2 tablespoons minced onions or shallots.

Prep time: 5 minutes | Cook time: 10 minutes | Serves 4 (2-OUNCE)

- 1 tablespoon olive oil
- 1 leek, white and green parts chopped
- 3 (2-ounce) freezer tray cubes white bean purée, thawed

1. In a large sauté pan, heat the olive oil on medium-high heat until it shimmers. Add the chopped leek and cook, stirring occasionally, until it's soft, 5 to 7 minutes.
2. Add the thawed white bean Purée to the sauté pan and mix the ingredients together. Continue cooking until just warmed. Store any unoffered Purée in the refrigerator for up to 3 days. Do not refreeze.

Sweet Potato, Chickpea, and Quinoa Purée

Chickpeas are soft and mash well, thus they serve as the meal's base. Cooked quinoa frozen in 2-ounce portions speeds up meal prep. Sweet potatoes sweeten quinoa and chickpeas' earthy aromas. Green bean or spinach Purée can be added to the chickpea Purée.

Prep time: 5 minutes | Cook time: 15 minutes | Serves 8 (2-ounce)

- 2 cups canned chickpeas, drained
- ⅛ teaspoon ground cinnamon
- ½ sweet potato, peeled and cut into ¼-inch dice, or 2 (2-ounce) freezer tray cubes sweet potato purée, thawed
- ½ cup cooked quinoa

1. In a blender or food processor, Purée the chickpeas and cinnamon until smooth. If needed, thin the Purée with breast milk, formula, or water to achieve the desired consistency.
2. If using thawed sweet potato, jump to step 3. If using fresh sweet potatoes, bring about 1 inch of water to a simmer in a small saucepan with a steamer insert. Place the sweet potatoes in the steamer insert. Cover and steam until tender, about 5 minutes. Allow to cool slightly.
3. In a small bowl, combine the Puréed chickpeas, sweet potato, and quinoa. If you like, gently warm a single serving of the mixture. Store any unoffered Purée in the refrigerator for up to 3 days or in the freezer for up to 6 months. Do not refreeze if using frozen sweet potato Purée.

Cranberry and Ground Beef Purée

Crumbled ground beef adds texture to stage 3 Purées. If the beef crumbles are too large, pulse them in a food processor or blender. Cook a pound of ground beef ahead of time and freeze 1/4-cup chunks for up to 6 months.

Prep time: 5 minutes | Cook time: 8 minutes | Serves 3 (2-ounce)

- 3 ounces ground beef
- ⅛ teaspoon dried thyme
- 3 (1-ounce) freezer tray cubes cranberry purée, thawed

1. In a small sauté pan, cook the ground beef over medium-high heat, crumbling it with a spoon, until brown, about 6 minutes. Add the thyme. Allow to cool slightly.
2. Stir the thawed cranberry Purée into the beef. Store any unoffered Purée in the refrigerator for up to 3 days. Do not refreeze.

Spinach, Black Bean, and Parsnip Purée

Cutting parsnips into bite-size pieces and boiling them until soft adds chunkiness to this Purée, while black beans and spinach provide protein and antioxidants.

Prep time: 5 minutes | Cook time: 10 minutes| Serves 4 (2-ounce)

- 1 parsnip, peeled and cut into ¼-inch dice
- 1 cup canned black beans, drained
- 3 (1-ounce) freezer tray cubes spinach purée, thawed
- ¼ cup cooked brown rice
-

1. In a blender or food processor, add the black beans and the thawed spinach Purée. Purée until smooth.
2. In a small saucepan with a steamer insert, bring about 1 inch of water to a simmer. Add the parsnip. Cover and steam until tender, about 5 minutes. Turn off the heat and remove the steamer insert with the parsnip. Pour out the cooking water, reserving it.
3. To the saucepan, add the parsnip, bean, and spinach Purée mixture, and brown rice. Stir to combine and heat on low until the Purée is warmed throughout. Thin, if necessary, with the reserved cooking water. Store any unoffered Purée in the refrigerator for up to 3 days. Do not refreeze.

Banana and Mango Purée

You can freeze extra parts of this sweet and luscious banana-mango Purée. Your baby will appreciate the sweet tropical flavors.

Prep time: 5 minutes | Cook time: 5 minutes| Serves 4 (2-ounce)

1 banana, peeled
1 mango, peeled, pitted, and cut into ¼-inch pieces

1. In a small bowl, mash the banana with a fork, thinning with breast milk, formula, or water as needed.
2. Stir in the mango pieces. Store any unoffered Purée in the refrigerator for up to 3 days or in the freezer for up to 6 months.

Pea, Quinoa, and Ground Turkey Purée

This recipe calls for fresh peas, but you may substitute pea Purée. Using frozen pea purée prevents refreezing.

Prep time: 5 minutes | Cook time: 25 minutes|Serves 8 (2-ounce)

- ½ cup quinoa
- 1 cup water
- ½ cup fresh or frozen peas
- ½ teaspoon minced fresh basil
- 4 ounces ground turkey

1. Using a fine-mesh sieve, run the quinoa under cold water to rinse. Drain.
2. In a small saucepan, bring the quinoa and 1 cup of water to a boil. Cover, reduce the heat to medium-low, and simmer for 12 minutes. Add the peas and simmer for 3 minutes more. Fluff with a fork and cool slightly.
3. Transfer half of the mixture to a food processor or blender. Add the basil and Purée until smooth. If needed, thin the Purée with breast milk, formula, nondairy milk, or water to achieve the desired consistency.
4. In a small sauté pan, cook the ground turkey over medium-high heat, crumbling it with a spoon, until brown, about 6 minutes. Allow to cool slightly.
5. Transfer the pea and quinoa mixture, the Purée, and the ground turkey to a medium bowl and stir to mix. Store any unoffered Purée in the refrigerator for up to 3 days or in the freezer for up to 6 months.

Parsnip, Carrot, and Lentil Purée

Instead of frozen vegetable Purées, cook 2 carrots and 2 parsnips. The extras are for snacking. Peel and quarter vegetables into sticks before baking in a 400°F oven. 30-minute roast.

Prep time: 5 minutes | Cook time: 5 minutes| Serves 4 (2-ounce)

- 3 (1-ounce) freezer tray cubes parsnip purée, thawed
- 3 (1-ounce) freezer tray cubes carrot purée, thawed
- ½ cup precooked lentils, drained if canned
- ¼ teaspoon dried tarragon

1. Combine the thawed Purées in a small saucepan. Add the lentils and the tarragon and mix well with a spoon.
2. Gently warm the Purée on the stove top over low heat. Store any unoffered Purée in the refrigerator for up to 3 days. Do not refreeze.

Zucchini, Yellow Squash, and Chicken Purée

This Purée uses summer squash like zucchini and yellow squash. Zucchini chunks are blended with chicken and squash Purées. As baby matures, switch to cooked veggies and meat. Zucchini adds chewiness to this chunky Purée, while butternut squash is sweet. Fiber, protein, and vitamin A are in this Purée.

Prep time: 5 minutes | Cook time: 5 minutes| Serves 4 (2-ounce)

- ¼ cup peeled diced zucchini (¼-inch dice)
- 3 (1-ounce) freezer tray cubes summer squash purée, thawed
- 2 (1-ounce) freezer tray cubes chicken purée, thawed

1. Combine the thawed Purées in a small saucepan. Mix well with a spoon. Gently warm the Purée over low heat.
2. In another small saucepan with a steamer insert, bring about 1 inch of water to a boil. Add the zucchini. Cover and simmer for 5 minutes.
3. Add the zucchini to the Purée and mix well with a spoon. Store any unoffered Purée in the refrigerator for up to 3 days. Do not refreeze.

Apricot, Sweet Potato, and Turkey Purée

Turkey and sweet potato is a classic pairing, and adding apricot brings out the sweet potato's sweetness, which complements the purée. This Purée contains vitamin A, which helps your baby's eyesight.

Prep time: 5 minutes | Cook time: 10 minutes| Serves 4 (2-ounce)

- 4 (1-ounce) freezer tray cubes sweet potato purée, thawed
- 2 (1-ounce) freezer tray cubes apricot purée, thawed
- ⅛ teaspoon ground ginger
- 2 ounces ground turkey

1. Combine the thawed Purées in a small saucepan. Add the ginger. Mix well with a spoon. Gently warm the Purée over low heat.
2. In a small sauté pan, cook the ground turkey, crumbling it with a spoon, until brown, about 6 minutes.
3. Add the turkey to the Purée and mix well with a spoon. Store any unoffered Purée in the refrigerator for up to 3 days. Do not refreeze.

Blueberry, Cottage Cheese, and Oat Cereal Purée

Cottage cheese is great for babies starting thick Purées. It provides protein and something to chew for your infant. Blueberries are antioxidant-rich, and oats are a complete grain. Looking for gluten-free oats?

Prep time: 5 minutes | Cook time: 5 minutes| Serves 3 (2-ounce)

- 2 (1-ounce) freezer tray cubes blueberry purée, thawed
- ¼ cup cottage cheese
- 2 (1-ounce) freezer tray cubes oat cereal, thawed
- 1/8 teaspoon ground cinnamon

1. In a small bowl, stir all the ingredients together until well combined.
2. Store any unoffered Purée in the refrigerator for up to 3 days. Do not refreeze.

Apple, Parsnip, and Spinach Purée

Apples and parsnips pair well raw (for older kids), cooked, or roasted. They sweeten spinach for a pleasant, healthy purée.

Prep time: 5 minutes | Cook time: 5 minutes| Serves 4 (2-ounce)

- ½ apple, peeled, cored, and cut into ¼-inch dice
- ½ parsnip, peeled and cut into ¼-inch dice
- 4 (1-ounce) freezer tray cubes spinach purée, thawed
- ¼ teaspoon ground cinnamon
- 2 (1-ounce) freezer tray cubes blueberry purée, thawed
- ¼ cup cottage cheese
- 2 (1-ounce) freezer tray cubes oat cereal, thawed
- ⅛ teaspoon ground cinnamon

1. In a saucepan with a steamer insert, bring about 1 inch of water to a simmer. Steam the apple and parsnip until very tender, about 10 minutes.
2. In a small bowl, combine the spinach Purée with the apples, parsnips, and cinnamon.
3. If desired, gently warm one serving of the Purée on the stove top over low heat. Store any unoffered Purée in the refrigerator for up to 3 days. Do not refreeze.

Cherry, Fig, and Salmon Purée

Cherries and figs pair well with omega-3-rich salmon. This Purée contains vitamin B12 and antioxidants. June and August/September are prime fig months.

Prep time: 5 minutes | Cook time: 10 minutes| Serves 4 (2-ounce)

- 2 ounces skinless salmon, cut into small pieces
- ¼ teaspoon minced fresh tarragon
- 1 fig, cut into ¼-inch dice
- 6 (1-ounce) freezer tray cubes cherry purée, thawed

1. Sprinkle the salmon with the tarragon.
2. In a small saucepan with a steamer insert, bring about 1 inch of water to a boil. Add the salmon and the figs. Steam until the fish is opaque, about 6 minutes.
3. Transfer the salmon and figs to a small bowl. Add the thawed cherry Purée. Mix well with a spoon to combine. Store any unoffered Purée in the refrigerator for up to 3 days. Do not refreeze.

Ground Pork and Apple Purée

Classic fall flavors include pork, apple, and sage. When cooking ground pork, crumble it using a spoon. If the pork is too large, pulse it in a food processor or blender.

Prep time: 5 minutes | Cook time: 5 minutes| Serves 4 (2-ounce)

- 2 ounces ground pork
- ⅛ teaspoon dried sage
- 6 (1-ounce) freezer tray cubes apple purée, thawed

1. Sprinkle the pork with the sage.
2. In a small sauté pan, cook the ground pork over medium-high heat, crumbling it with a spoon, until brown, about 6 minutes.
3. Transfer the pork to a small bowl and add the thawed apple Purée. Mix well with a spoon to combine. Store any unoffered Purée in the refrigerator for up to 3 days. Do not refreeze.

Beef, Blackberry, and Brown Rice Purée

Blackberry is delicious with meat and herbs. Precooked organic rice in the freezer or rice area speeds up cooking times. Freeze cooked rice in 14-cup quantities in zip-top bags for 6 months.

Prep time: 5 minutes | Cook time: 5 minutes| Serves 4 (2-ounce)

- 3 (1-ounce) freezer tray cubes blackberry purée, thawed
- 2 (1-ounce) freezer tray cubes beef purée, thawed
- ¼ cup cooked brown rice
- ¼ teaspoon dried thyme

1. Combine the thawed Purées in a small bowl. Add the rice and thyme. Mix well with a spoon.
2. Gently warm a single serving of the mixture. Store any unoffered Purée in the refrigerator for up to 3 days. Do not refreeze.

Broccoli, Onion, and Quinoa Purée

Cooked quinoa makes making Purées easy. You can thaw quinoa with Purées in the fridge, gently rewarming them together.

Prep time: 5 minutes | Cook time: 15 minutes| Serves 4 (2-ounce)

- 1 tablespoon olive oil
- ½ onion, minced
- 4 (1-ounce) freezer tray cubes broccoli purée, thawed
- ¼ cup cooked quinoa

1. In a medium sauté pan, heat the olive oil on medium-high heat until it shimmers. Add the onion and cook, stirring occasionally, until soft, about 7 minutes.
2. Add the broccoli Purée and quinoa and mix all of the ingredients. Continue cooking until the mixture is warm, 2 to 3 minutes. Store any unoffered Purée in the refrigerator for up to 3 days. Do not refreeze.

Pomegranate-Banana-Berry Purée

As newborns become older, their digestive systems get stronger, so you no longer need to prepare fruits. This is a Purée-and-serve recipe. Purée poured into freezer pop molds provides a healthful teething delight.

Prep time: 5 minutes| Cook time: 5 minutes| Serves 4 (½-cup)

- 1 medium banana
- ¼ cup pomegranate juice
- 1 cup fresh or frozen blueberries, rinsed

1. Combine the banana, pomegranate juice, and blueberries in a blender or food processor and Purée until smooth, pausing to scrape down any large chunks from the sides of the bowl.
2. If you are using frozen berries and you plan on freezing this Purée for later use, you will have to cook the blueberries first. For food safety purposes, frozen food must first be cooked before it gets refrozen.

Sautéed Kale and Summer Squash Purée

Garlic! Garlic helps babies nurse better, but we adore it for its cold-fighting properties. Garlic's antibacterial and antiviral qualities help baby's stuffy nose.

Prep time: 5 minutes| Cook time: 15 minutes| Serves 8 (½-cup)

- 4 tablespoons extra-virgin olive oil, divided
- 2 garlic cloves, minced
- 1½ cups fresh baby kale
- 1 pound zucchini or summer squash, cut into ½-inch rounds
- ¼ teaspoon dried oregano
- 2 tablespoons grated Parmesan cheese (optional)

1. In a large skillet over medium heat, heat 2 tablespoons of oil. Add the garlic and let it heat for 1 minute.
2. Carefully add the kale and sauté for 3 to 5 minutes until wilted, tossing occasionally with tongs. Use a rubber spatula to transfer the kale to a food processor.
3. In the same pan, pour the remaining 2 tablespoons of olive oil. Add the zucchini in a single layer, sprinkle evenly with the oregano, and let cook for 2 minutes without moving it around the pan. Use a rubber spatula to flip the zucchini and cook for 2 to 3 minutes more until golden on both sides.
4. Using a rubber spatula, add the zucchini to the food processor with the kale.
5. Add the Parmesan cheese (if using) and Purée until smooth.

Roasted Root Vegetable Purée

Single-layer roasting produces beautiful, caramelized root vegetables. Avoid piling vegetables on the baking sheet to prevent steaming. Parchment paper simplifies cleanup.

Prep time: 5 minutes| Cook time: 40 minutes| Serves 8 (½-cup)

- ¼ cup extra-virgin olive oil
- 4 cups mixed root vegetables (choose from sweet potatoes, butternut squash, rutabaga, carrots, parsnips, Brussels sprouts, and acorn squash), peeled and diced into 2-inch pieces
- 1 medium onion, thickly chopped
- 3 thyme sprigs
- 3 garlic cloves, peeled

1. Preheat the oven to 400°F. Line two large baking sheets with parchment paper.
2. In a large bowl, toss together the olive oil, root vegetables, onion, thyme, and garlic. Spread in an even layer on the baking sheets (use the second baking sheet if the first doesn't fit all the vegetables in one layer).
3. Cook for 40 minutes until the vegetables are golden brown. Remove the thyme stems, then transfer the vegetables to a food processor. Purée until smooth, adding water if needed to achieve the desired consistency.

Cherry and Coconut Cream Purée

Using pitted frozen cherries makes this Purée year-round, not only during the brief cherry season. This delightful purée is hard to resist.

Prep time: 5 minutes| Cook time: 5 minutes| Serves 5 (½-cup)

- 1 (12-ounce) bag frozen pitted dark sweet cherries, thawed
- 1 cup pure coconut cream
- 5 fresh mint leaves

1. Combine the cherries, cream, and mint in a blender and Purée until completely smooth.

Peaches and Cream Smoothie

This smoothie provides energy from oats, fiber and minerals from fruit, and bone-building protein from yogurt. Frozen peaches thicken and creamify the drink, saving time on busy mornings.

Prep time: 5 minutes| Cook time: 5 minutes| Serves 5 (½-cup)

- 1 cup milk of choice
- ½ cup vanilla Greek or Icelandic yogurt
- 1 cup frozen peach slices
- ⅓ cup old-fashioned rolled oats
- ⅛ teaspoon ground cinnamon

1. Combine the milk, yogurt, peaches, oats, and cinnamon in a blender and Purée until completely smooth.
2. To serve, pour the smoothie into a sippy cup or baby food pouch, or serve from a spoon. Leftover smoothies can be frozen in baby food trays or pouches.

Baby'S First Green Smoothie

When my oldest refused vegetables, I made him this smoothie every morning. It was nice to know that he always started the day with fruit, vegetables, and protein. A smoothie is a safe way to introduce nuts to children. If your child has a nut or seed allergy, omit it.

Prep time: 5 minutes| Cook time: 50 minutes| Serves 5 (½-cup)

- 1½ cups milk of choice
- 1 cup (unpacked) baby spinach
- 1 ripe banana
- 1 heaping tablespoon smooth peanut butter
- 1 heaping tablespoon raw cacao powder

1. Combine the milk, spinach, banana, peanut butter, and cacao powder in a blender and Purée until completely smooth.
2. To serve, pour the smoothie into a sippy cup or baby food pouch, or serve from a spoon.

Baked Apples with Pears and Cinnamon

This apple-pear bake smells as good as apple pie yet is healthy enough for breakfast. Save a scoop for breakfast with yogurt and granola, dinner with pork chops, or dessert with vanilla ice cream.

Prep time: 5 minutes| Cook time: 60 minutes| Serves 5 (½-cup)

- 2 tablespoons unsalted butter, divided
- 4 medium apples, peeled, cored, and sliced
- 4 medium pears, peeled, cored, and sliced
- 1 teaspoon ground cinnamon

- ½ teaspoon ground nutmeg
- ¼ teaspoon ground cardamom
- ¼ cup apple cider

1. Preheat the oven to 375°F. Grease a 9-by-12-inch glass baking dish with 1 tablespoon of butter.
2. In a medium bowl, toss together the apples, pears, cinnamon, nutmeg, cardamom, and apple cider. Pour this mixture into the baking dish, spread it out evenly, and top with the remaining 1 tablespoon of butter. Cover with aluminum foil and bake for 45 minutes to 1 hour, until the apples and pears are fork-tender.
3. Using a slotted spoon, transfer the apples and pears to a food processor and Purée until smooth, adding liquid from the baking dish if needed to achieve your desired consistency.

Slow Cooker Bone Broth

During flu season, I make this broth once a month. Bone broth includes protein and minerals and helps prevent colds and flu. Give it to your youngster in a sippy cup or freeze it in cubes to incorporate into Purées. Wash everything before chopping it, even the onion, which can be left unpeeled. Vinegar helps take out nutrients from the bones, and you won't taste it.

Prep time: 5 minutes| Cook time: 18 hours | Serves 16 (½-cup)

- 3 to 4 pounds chicken or beef bones
- 2 large carrots, peeled and chopped into thirds
- 3 celery stalks, chopped into thirds
- 1 large onion, halved
- Handful of fresh herb sprigs (such as parsley, dill, rosemary, thyme, or a combination)
- 2 tablespoons apple cider vinegar

1. In the slow cooker combine the chicken or beef bones, carrots, celery, onion, herbs, and vinegar. Add enough water to cover everything.
2. Cook on low for 12 to 18 hours.
3. Using a fine-mesh strainer, strain the broth into a large heatproof bowl and discard the vegetables and the bones. Let the broth cool. (It may turn gelatinous when cold—that's all the good-for-you collagen from the bones.)

Mashed Potatoes and Parsnips

Parsnips give mashed potatoes a zest. The "no milk before age 1" restriction only applies to bottle feeding because cow's milk doesn't contain enough nutrients to replace breast milk or formula. You can replace whole milk with a milk replacement or low-sodium chicken stock if you wish.

Prep time: 5 minutes| Cook time: 30 minutes| Serves 8 (½-cup)

- 2 pounds (about 4 medium) russet potatoes, chopped
- ½ pound (about 3 medium) parsnips, peeled and chopped
- 4 tablespoons (½ stick) unsalted butter
- 3 garlic cloves, minced
- 1 rosemary sprig
- ¾ cup whole milk

1. In a medium saucepan, cover the potatoes and parsnips with water. Bring to a boil over medium-high heat, then reduce the heat to medium-low and simmer until the potatoes are fork-tender, about 20 minutes. Drain the vegetables and set aside.
2. In that same saucepan, melt the butter over medium-low heat. Add the garlic and rosemary sprig and cook, swirling the pan until the butter is melted, about 5 minutes. Turn off the heat and use tongs to remove and discard the rosemary.
3. Add the potatoes, parsnips, and milk to the butter. Mash with a potato masher or use an immersion blender to beat until smooth and creamy, adding more milk if desired. For adults, season to taste with salt and pepper.

Roasted Beets with Orange And Ginger

Ginger and orange zest spice up roasted beets. Beet juice stains clothes and fingers, so wear an apron. Baking soda and water will remove purple off your fingers.

Prep time: 5 minutes| Cook time: 60 minutes| Serves 6 (½-cup)

- 4 beets (about 1 pound)
- Grated zest of 1 orange
- 1 teaspoon grated fresh ginger

1. Preheat the oven to 400°F. Line a large, rimmed baking sheet with parchment paper or aluminum foil (to help catch beet juice spills).
2. Cut off the beet greens and save them for another use. (They're yummy sautéed.) Rinse the beets well under running water. Wrap each beet in foil and place them all on the baking sheet. Roast for 40 to 60 minutes, checking for doneness by piercing the foil with a fork or knife. Once they're tender all the way through, remove the beets from the oven and let them cool for 15 minutes

before unwrapping.
3. To peel the beets, hold them in paper towels and rub off the skins. Chop the peeled beets into quarters.
4. In a food processor, combine the beets, orange zest, and ginger. Purée until smooth, adding water if necessary to create the desired consistency.

Roasted Butternut Squash with Fennel and Ginger

This butternut squash is delicious! Roasting vegetables enhances their sweetness. Ginger helps stomach disturbances, and fennel is a natural colic treatment and laxative. Non-vegans and vegetarians can use low-sodium chicken stock.

Prep time: 5 minutes| Cook time: 30 minutes| Serves 10 (½-cup)

- 1 medium butternut squash, peeled, seeded, and cut into 1-inch chunks
- 1 fennel bulb, green parts removed and discarded, cut into 2-inch chunks
- 3 tablespoons extra-virgin olive oil, divided
- 1 medium onion, chopped
- 1 garlic clove, minced
- 2 cups low-sodium vegetable stock
- ½ teaspoon ground ginger

1. Preheat the oven to 425°F. Line a large, rimmed baking sheet with parchment paper. Spread the squash and fennel in a single layer on the baking sheet, then drizzle with 1 tablespoon of oil. Roast for 25 minutes or until the squash begins to turn golden brown. Remove the baking sheet from the oven.
2. Heat the remaining 2 tablespoons of oil in a medium stockpot over medium-high heat. Add the onion and sauté until soft and translucent, about 5 minutes. Add the garlic and sauté for 1 minute more.
3. To the stockpot, add the roasted vegetables, stock, and ginger. Bring to a boil, reduce the heat to medium-low, and simmer for 10 minutes.
4. Use an immersion blender to Purée the cooked vegetable mixture until smooth, or transfer the cooled mixture to a food processor or blender and blend until completely smooth.

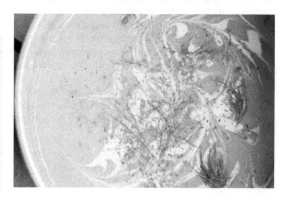

Spring Peas with Mint

Peas and mint are as classic as PB&J. This recipe can be served cold with crème fraîche or whole-milk yogurt. Adults can eat it with grilled chicken or fish.

Prep time: 5 minutes| Cook time: 10 minutes| Serves 10 (½-cup)

- 2 tablespoons extra-virgin olive oil
- 1 medium onion, diced
- 1 cup low-sodium vegetable stock
- 2 (10-ounce) bags frozen peas
- 1 tablespoon chopped fresh basil leaves
- 1 tablespoon chopped fresh mint leaves

1. In a large saucepan over medium heat, combine the oil and onion. Sauté, stirring occasionally, until the onion is soft and translucent, about 5 minutes.
2. Add the stock, increase the heat to medium-high, and bring to a low boil. Add the peas and cook for 2 minutes, stirring occasionally. Turn off the heat and stir in the basil and mint.
3. Let the pea mixture cool slightly. Working in batches, transfer the mixture to a blender or food processor and Purée until smooth.

Curry Roasted Cauliflower Purée

This healthful recipe uses turmeric. This gold-colored spice is known for its antioxidant, anti-inflammatory, and antibacterial effects. Set aside some cauliflower before putting it in the food processor. Salt, pepper, and lemon juice.

Prep time: 5 minutes| Cook time: 30 minutes| Serves 8 (½-cup)

- 1 medium head cauliflower, cut into florets
- 1 small white onion, coarsely chopped
- ¼ cup extra-virgin olive oil
- 1 teaspoon curry powder
- ½ teaspoon ground turmeric

1. Preheat the oven to 400°F. Line a large, rimmed baking sheet with parchment paper.
2. Combine the cauliflower and onion on the baking sheet. Drizzle the vegetables with the olive oil and sprinkle with the curry and turmeric. Use a wooden spoon to stir the vegetables to coat them evenly, then spread them into one even layer.
3. Roast for 25 minutes or until the cauliflower begins to turn golden brown.
4. Let the vegetables cool slightly, then carefully transfer them to a food processor. Purée until smooth, adding water as necessary to achieve the desired consistency.

Coconut Whipped Sweet Potatoes

Coconut milk makes these sweet potatoes thick, creamy, and flavorful. Coconut includes iron, magnesium, zinc, vitamins C and E, which strengthen bone strength and boost the immune system.

Prep time: 5 minutes| Cook time: 20 minutes| Serves 8 (½-cup)

- 2 pounds (about 4 medium) sweet potatoes, peeled and chopped
- 1 teaspoon ground cinnamon
- 1 (14.5-ounce) can full-fat coconut milk

1. Put the sweet potatoes in a large saucepan and pour in enough water to cover them by 1 to 2 inches. Place the pan over high heat. Bring the water to a boil, then reduce the heat to medium-low and cook until the potatoes are fork-tender, about 15 minutes.
2. Drain the potatoes and place them in a deep bowl with the cinnamon. Using an immersion blender or potato masher, mash the potatoes until smooth, slowly pouring in the coconut milk as you go. If necessary, add water to create a smoother Purée.

Sautéed Ground Beef and Vegetables

Beef includes easily absorbed iron, which is crucial because a baby's iron levels dip around 6 months. Here, ground beef is further broken down. Beef never entirely Purées.

Prep time: 5 minutes| Cook time: 10 minutes| Serves 10 (½-cup)

- 1 pound ground beef
- 2 tablespoons extra-virgin olive oil
- 1 red bell pepper, seeded and diced
- 1 small onion, diced
- 1 garlic clove, minced
- 1 heaping teaspoon ground cumin

1. In a large sauté pan over medium heat, cook the beef in the oil until browned, breaking apart the meat with a wooden spoon.
2. Add the bell pepper and onion and sauté until the vegetables are soft, about 5 minutes. Add the garlic and cumin and cook for 1 minute more.
3. Carefully transfer the slightly cooled meat mixture to a food processor and pulse until finely ground, adding water or stock if needed to achieve your desired consistency.

One-Pan Roasted Chicken Dinner

Sheet-pan dinners win weeknights. After some prep, everything is baked on one sheet for simple cleanup. This style of chicken supper is fuss-free.

Prep time: 5 minutes| Cook time: 35 minutes| Serves 12 (½-cup)

- 1¼ pounds boneless, skinless chicken thighs, chopped into 2-inch pieces
- 1 pound (about 4 medium) carrots, peeled and cut into 2-inch-long chunks
- 1 pound (about 4 medium) parsnips, peeled and cut into 2-inch-long chunks
- 1 pound baby potatoes, quartered
- 3 tablespoons extra-virgin olive oil
- 2 teaspoons fresh thyme leaves
- Grated zest of 1 lemon
- ½ teaspoon garlic powder
- ½ teaspoon onion powder
- 1 cup low-sodium chicken stock

1. Preheat the oven to 375°F. Line a large, rimmed baking sheet with parchment paper.
2. Spread the chicken, carrots, parsnips, and potatoes on the baking sheet. Drizzle with the olive oil and then sprinkle with the thyme, lemon zest, and garlic and onion powders. Toss the ingredients together. Spread the mixture in a single layer and bake until the chicken is no longer pink (with an internal temperature of 165°F) and the carrots and potatoes are fork-tender, 25 to 35 minutes.
3. Let the mixture cool slightly. Carefully transfer half of the mixture to a food processor. Pulse until smooth, adding the chicken stock as needed to thin the mixture to your desired consistency. Repeat with the other half of the mixture or save it for yourself.

Mango-Banana Nice Cream

First ice cream without cream or sugar. Frozen bananas become smooth and creamy after being processed. Mango chunks add a tropical flavor. It's awesome!

Prep time: 50 minutes| Cook time: 20 minutes| Serves 4 (½-cup)

- 2 large ripe bananas
- ½ cup frozen mango chunks

1. Line a large, rimmed baking sheet with parchment paper. Peel the bananas, cut them into rounds, and place them on the baking sheet. Freeze until firm, a minimum of 2 hours. (Frozen banana slices can be stored in a sealed container in the freezer for up to 2 months.)
2. Combine the frozen banana and mango in a food processor. Purée until smooth and creamy, pausing to scrape down the sides of the bowl once or twice. Serve immediately.

Pumpkin Pie Purée

This sweet Purée has two superfoods and pumpkin pie flavor. Serve with a spoon, keep in a baby food pouch, or blend it into a smoothie. Most people prefer cold smoothies (include ice before blending), but babies prefer room-temperature foods.

Prep time: 5 minutes| Cook time: 5 minutes| Serves 9 (½-cup)

- 2 bananas, peeled and chopped
- 1 cup plain whole-milk yogurt
- 1 cup canned pumpkin purée
- ½ cup carrot juice
- ⅛ teaspoon ground cinnamon
- ⅛ teaspoon pumpkin pie spice

1. Combine all the ingredients in a food processor or blender and Purée until completely smooth.

Chapter 5
Smoothies and Finger Foods(10 Months and Up)

Foods in stage four are served to the baby after it masters stage three Purées. The baby is served with bigger chunks of food which you give it to it at different times as you do not want to overload it with too much food. Finger foods shouldn't be fed any earlier than this stage as by now your baby can chew, sit properly and lift food from its plate. It is a good idea to investing in a nice high chair, a mat to put under the high chair, a suction plate, self-feeding spoons and a long-sleeved bib. It is also important to understand how to prepare finger foods and smoothies and ensure they are soft. The food should be soft enough to squish between your two fingers. Soft food enables chewing and swallowing. Consider what method you are going to use to prepare the meal, and avoid fats and oils. Hard fruits and vegetables should be steamed or roasted. Make sure you serve the food in the right size as you do not your baby choking. If you realize your baby is it becomes quiet, the skin turns color to blue, and it cannot cry or make any sound. If this happens you many consider infant CPR.

Broccoli Trees with Avocado Dip

Steam extra broccoli to save time. Refrigerate for up to 3 days and serve with avocado dip, Spinach Pesto, or in a salad.

Prep time: 5 minutes | Cook time: 5 minutes| Makes about ½ cup avocado dip

- ½ cup broccoli florets
- ½ avocado
- 2 tablespoons plain greek yogurt
- 2 tablespoons mayonnaise
- 1 teaspoon lime juice

1. In a medium saucepan, bring 2 inches of water to a simmer. Place a steamer basket over the water. Add the broccoli florets. Cover and steam until tender, about 5 minutes. Transfer to a plate.
2. Add the avocado, yogurt, mayonnaise, and lime juice to a food processor or blender. Process until smooth, adding a tablespoon or more water if needed to help it blend. Serve 2 tablespoons avocado dip with the broccoli.

Sweet-and-Sour Tofu Sticks

Introduce your baby to high-protein tofu early and it may become one of your culinary MVPs. Warm, room temperature, or cold, these tofu sticks are excellent. They're jiggly when hot, then firm up as they cool.

Prep time: 5 minutes | Cook time: 55 minutes| Makes 12 sticks

- 1 lb. extra-firm tofu, drained
- 1 tablespoon maple syrup
- 1 tablespoon low-sodium soy sauce
- 1 tablespoon rice vinegar
- 2 tablespoons sesame oil
- ¼ teaspoon sesame seeds, white or black

1. Place the tofu block on a plate lined with a few folded paper towels. Cover the tofu with more folded paper towels. Place another plate on top and weigh down the plate with something heavy, like a can of tomatoes. Let the tofu drain for 20 minutes. Slice the tofu into 12 sticks and transfer to a large, flat baking dish.
2. In a small bowl, whisk together the maple syrup, soy sauce, rice vinegar, and sesame oil. Pour over the tofu sticks and turn to coat. Let marinate for up to an hour, turning once.
3. Preheat the oven to 400°F. Line a rimmed baking sheet with parchment paper. Transfer the tofu sticks to the parchment paper, pouring any marinade over the top. Sprinkle with sesame seeds and bake for 30 minutes.

Smoky Squash Cakes

This vegetable pancake is perfect for infants and toddlers. Butternut squash is a great source of vitamin A, which is great for your health.

Prep time: 5 minutes | Cook time: 5 minutes| Makes 12 patties

- 1 cup butternut squash purée
- 1 egg, beaten
- ½ cup panko breadcrumbs
- 1 scallion, finely chopped
- 2 tablespoons chopped cilantro
- ¾ teaspoon cumin
- 1 tablespoon olive oil, plus more if necessary

1. In a medium-sized bowl, combine all of the ingredients except for the olive oil. Form into 12 patties.
2. Heat 1 tablespoon olive oil in a large skillet over medium-high heat. Sauté the patties until golden brown, about 3 minutes per side, cooking in batches if necessary to avoid overcrowding.

Maple Graham Animals

Avoid animal crackers with trans fat and high-fructose corn syrup. Cut this gently sweetened whole-grain dough. Circles and stars are just as cute as animal-shaped crackers.

Prep time: 5 minutes | Cook time: 15 minutes| Makes about 60 small crackers

- ½ cup whole-wheat graham flour or whole-wheat flour
- ½ cup all-purpose flour, plus more for dusting
- ½ teaspoon baking powder
- ½ teaspoon cinnamon
- ⅛ teaspoon salt
- ¼ cup unsalted butter, softened
- 2 tablespoons milk
- 2 tablespoons maple syrup

1. Preheat the oven to 375°F. Line a rimmed baking sheet with parchment paper.
2. In a large bowl, whisk together the two flours, baking powder, cinnamon, and salt. Using an electric mixer, beat in the butter, milk, and maple syrup just until a stiff dough forms.
3. Sprinkle a clean work surface with flour. Transfer the dough to the work surface and roll it out to ¼-inch thickness. Using small cookie cutters (about 1½ inches wide), cut shapes from the dough and place them on the baking sheet. Re-roll and cut the remaining dough. Bake for 12 to 14 minutes or until golden brown.

Miso-Sesame Sweet Potatoes

These sweet potato wedges are soft, sweet, and nutty. The glaze keeps indefinitely, so make a double batch to use on fish, salad dressing, steamed vegetables, or straight from the spoon.

Prep time: 5 minutes | Cook time: 55 minutes| Makes about 8 servings

- 3 large sweet potatoes
- ⅓ cup white miso paste
- ⅔ cup tahini (sesame seed paste)
- ¾ cup water
- ¼ cup apple juice
- 3 tablespoons maple syrup

1. Preheat the oven to 400°F. Line a rimmed baking sheet with parchment paper.
2. Cut the sweet potatoes into ½-inch thick wedges and set aside in a large bowl.
3. In a small bowl, combine the miso, tahini, water, apple juice, and maple syrup and whisk until completely blended. Pour about half of the miso mixture over the sweet potatoes and toss to coat evenly.
4. Lay the potatoes in a single layer on the prepared baking sheet. Roast for 40 to 45 minutes, until browned. Serve warm or at room temperature, with extra sauce drizzled on top or served on the side as a dip.

Pasta with Spinach Pesto

Make a note of this recipe. You'll want to keep making this pesto long after your child has moved on from the stage of eating finger foods.

Prep time: 5 minutes | Cook time: 5 minutes| Makes 1 cup pesto

FOR PESTO:
- one 5-oz. package baby spinach
- 2 cups basil, packed
- ¼ cup walnuts, lightly toasted
- ¼ cup grated parmesan cheese
- 1 small clove garlic
- ½ cup olive oil
- For serving:
- ¼ cup cooked whole-grain penne pasta

1. Bring a medium pot of water to a boil. Add the spinach and cook for 15 seconds. Drain well, squeezing out any water with a fork.
2. Add all of the pesto ingredients, including the spinach, to a food processor and process until smooth. To serve, mix 2 teaspoons pesto with ¼ cup cooked pasta, or serve the pesto as a dip.

Cornmeal and Zucchini Pancakes

As a dipping sauce, you can choose to use Greek yogurt, sour cream, or applesauce with these nutritious pancakes.

Prep time: 5 minutes | Cook time: 5 minutes| Makes about 24 pancakes

- 2 large zucchini, grated (about 5 cups)
- ¼ cup finely chopped scallions
- 2 large eggs
- 1½ cups shredded cheddar cheese
- ¾ cup milk
- freshly ground pepper, to taste
- 2 cups cornmeal
- 1 teaspoon baking powder
- 2 tablespoons olive oil

1. Wrap the grated zucchini in a clean towel, and squeeze out as much moisture as possible.
2. In a large bowl, combine the zucchini, scallions, eggs, cheese, milk, and pepper to taste. In a small bowl, stir together the cornmeal and baking powder. Add the dry ingredients to the zucchini mixture and stir to combine.
3. Heat 1 tablespoon of olive oil in a large skillet over medium-high heat. When the oil is hot, drop the batter into the pan by the tablespoonful. Cook for about 3 minutes on the first side, until the pancakes start to look set around the edges and the bottoms are golden. Flip and cook for about 2 minutes more. Place the cooked pancakes on a paper towel-lined plate and repeat with the remaining oil and batter.

Yogurt Berry Smoothie

Smoothies are a pleasant way to give your infant healthful meals. You may use frozen fruit Purée cubes to make this traditional smoothie in the spring. Protein-rich yogurt.

Prep time: 5 minutes | Cook time: 5 minutes| Makes 2 (1-cup)

- 3 (1-ounce) freezer tray cubes berry purée, thawed, or 3 ounces berries of your choice
- 2 (1-ounce) freezer tray cubes spinach or kale purée, thawed
- 2 ounces plain full-fat yogurt (nondairy if desired)
- 3 ounces breast milk, formula, or any nondairy milk
- ⅛ teaspoon ground cinnamon

1. In a blender, combine all the ingredients. Process until the mixture is smooth.
2. Store any unoffered smoothie in the refrigerator for up to 3 days. When serving the remaining smoothie, adjust the consistency with a little extra liquid as needed and blend again before serving.

Polenta Diamonds

These chunky sticks are ideal for children's hands since they are simple to pick up and then submerge in sour tomato sauce.

Prep time: 5 minutes | Cook time: 45 minutes| Makes 12 diamonds

- 1½ cups water
- ½ cup quick-cooking polenta
- 1 tablespoon unsalted butter

FOR SERVING:
- ¼ cup go-to tomato sauce

1. In a medium saucepan over high heat, bring the water to a boil. Pour in the polenta in a smooth stream, whisking all the while to prevent lumps. Turn the heat to low and simmer the polenta until thickened and smooth, 3 to 5 minutes, stirring frequently.
2. Fit a large piece of parchment paper into an 8 x 8 baking dish, leaving the parchment overhanging the sides like handles. Pour the polenta into the dish, spreading it with a spatula until even. Let cool for 30 minutes.
3. Preheat the oven to 350°F. Lift the parchment out of the baking dish and place it on a cutting board. Cut the polenta into 12 diamonds or rectangles. Transfer the parchment to a baking sheet. Spread out the diamonds and bake for 10 minutes.
4. Serve the diamonds with Go-To Tomato Sauce for dipping.

Carrot Cake Smoothie

This dessert favorite becomes a creamy drink. The date's sweetness makes extra sugars unnecessary. Enjoy anytime!

Prep time: 5 minutes | Cook time: 5 minutes|Serves 2 (1-cup)

- 1 cup breast milk, formula, or any nondairy milk
- ½ frozen banana
- ½ cup sliced carrot
- 1 medjool date, pitted
- 1 tablespoon nut butter of choice
- 1 teaspoon chia seeds
- 1 teaspoon cinnamon

1. In a blender, combine all the ingredients. Process until smooth. Store any unoffered smoothie in the refrigerator for up to 3 days.
2. When serving the remaining smoothie, adjust the consistency with a little extra liquid as needed and blend again before serving.

Mini Maple BBQ Turkey Meatloaf Bites

Suzy Scherr, a personal chef friend, shared this dish. Her kids enjoy these little, protein-packed meatloaves. Use your family's favorite ground meat.

Prep time: 5 minutes | Cook time: 40 minutes| Makes 24 meatloaves

- ⅔ cup ketchup
- 6 tablespoons maple syrup
- 1½ tablespoons white wine vinegar
- 1½ tablespoons worcestershire sauce
- 2 teaspoons paprika
- pinch cayenne (optional)
- 1 egg
- 1 lb. ground turkey (preferably 94% lean)
- ½ cup dried bread crumbs
- 1 tablespoon onion powder
- 1 tablespoon garlic powder

1. Preheat the oven to 350°F. Lightly grease a 24-cup mini muffin pan with cooking spray or insert liners.
2. In a small bowl, make the BBQ sauce by combining the ketchup, maple syrup, vinegar, Worcestershire, paprika, and cayenne, if using. Mix well and set aside.
3. Crack the egg in a large bowl and beat it with a fork. Add the ground turkey, breadcrumbs, onion and garlic powders, and half the BBQ sauce. Mix well. Divide the turkey mixture evenly among the muffin cups. Brush the tops with the remaining BBQ sauce.
4. Bake for 25 to 30 minutes or until the internal temperature of each meatloaf reaches 165°F when tested with an instant-read thermometer.

Fruity Spinach and Avocado Smoothie

This delightful smoothie contains nutritious spinach. Spinach is high in A, B6, C, and iron, while kiwi is strong in fiber and C. Pear sweetens the smoothie.

Prep time: 5 minutes | Cook time: 5 minutes|Serves 2 (1-cup)

- 4 ounces breast milk, formula, or any nondairy milk
- 1 kiwi, peeled
- 2 (1-ounce) freezer tray cubes pear purée, thawed
- 4 (1-ounce) freezer tray cubes spinach purée, thawed, or 4 ounces frozen spinach
- ½ avocado, pitted
- 1 tablespoon fresh mint or basil (optional)

1. In a blender, combine all the ingredients. Process until smooth. Store any unoffered smoothie in the refrigerator for up to 3 days.
2. When serving the remaining smoothie, adjust the consistency with a little extra liquid as needed and blend again before serving.

Pumpkin Smoothie

Using canned pumpkin makes this smoothie easy and no-cook, but use frozen pumpkin Purée if you have it. If you don't have hemp seeds, 1 cup of yogurt will do. This smoothie tastes like pumpkin pie year-round.

Prep time: 5 minutes | Cook time: 5 minutes|Serves 2 (1-cup)

- 6 ounces breast milk,or any nondairy milk
- 1 cup pumpkin purée, thawed, or canned pumpkin
- ¼ cup crushed ice
- ½ teaspoon pumpkin pie seasoning
- 1 tablespoon hemp seeds

1. In a blender, combine all the ingredients. Process until smooth. Store any unoffered smoothie in the refrigerator for up to 3 days.
2. When serving the remaining smoothie, adjust the consistency with a little extra liquid as needed and blend again before serving.

Almond Butter and Cherry Smoothie

This smoothie is like a PB&J with almonds and juicy cherries. It's meaty and delicious, and fresh (nondairy) milk goes directly into the smoothie.

Prep time: 5 minutes | Cook time: 5 minutes|Serves 2 (1-cup)

- 6 ounces breast milk, formula, or any nondairy milk
- 2 tablespoons almond butter
- 4 (1-ounce) freezer tray cubes cherry purée, thawed

1. In a blender, combine all the ingredients. Process until smooth. Store any unoffered smoothie in the refrigerator for up to 3 days.
2. When serving the remaining smoothie, adjust the consistency with a little extra liquid as needed and blend again before serving.

Protein Power Smoothie

This recipe uses a couple of ounces of tofu to pack in protein without sacrificing taste. Banana and butternut squash make a delightful and healthful pairing for your child.

Prep time: 5 minutes | Cook time: 5 minutes|Serves 2 (1-cup)

- 6 ounces breast milk, formula, or any nondairy milk
- 2 ounces tofu
- 2 (1-ounce) freezer tray cubes butternut squash Purée, thawed
- ½ banana, peeled
- ¼ teaspoon ground ginger

1. In a blender, combine all the ingredients. Process until smooth. Store any unoffered smoothie in the refrigerator for up to 3 days.
2. When serving the remaining smoothie, adjust the consistency with a little extra liquid as needed and blend again before serving.

Kale and Mango Smoothie

Juicy mangoes with a large pit might be difficult to cut. To cut a mango, peel it and slice lengthwise around the pit to separate the flesh. Cut around the pit into cubes.

Prep time: 5 minutes | Cook time: 5 minutes|Serves 2 (1-cup)

- 6 ounces breast milk, formula, or any nondairy milk
- ½ mango, peeled, pitted, and cut into cubes
- 3 (1-ounce) freezer tray cubes kale purée, thawed
- ¼ teaspoon ground allspice

1. In a blender, combine all the ingredients. Process until smooth. Store any unoffered smoothie in the refrigerator for up to 3 days.
2. When serving the remaining smoothie, adjust the consistency with a little extra liquid as needed and blend again before serving.

Banana Cream Pie Smoothie

This naturally sweet blend combines frozen banana, vanilla, and nutmeg. Turmeric is anti-inflammatory and kefir has protein and probiotics.

Prep time: 5 minutes | Cook time: 5 minutes|Serves 2 (1-CUP)

- 4 ounces breast milk, or any nondairy milk
- 1 cup plain yogurt (nondairy if desired) or unsweetened kefir
- 1 small frozen banana
- ½ teaspoon pure vanilla extract
- 1 teaspoon ground turmeric
- 1 teaspoon allspice or nutmeg
- ¼ cup ice

1. In a blender, combine all the ingredients. Process until smooth. Store any unoffered smoothie in the refrigerator for up to 3 days.
2. When serving the remaining smoothie, adjust the consistency with a little extra liquid as needed and blend again before serving.

Mixed Berry Smoothie Bowl

Smoothie bowls are popular with adults, but babies who can't use a straw love them, too. Juicy berries and yogurt create the smoothie's base, and toppings add flavor. Mix in toppings your baby can chew and swallow.

Prep time: 5 minutes | Cook time: 15 minutes|Serves 2 (1-cup)

FOR THE SMOOTHIE
- 2 ounces breast milk, formula, or any nondairy milk
- ½ cup frozen blueberries
- ½ cup frozen strawberries
- 1 cup plain yogurt (nondairy if desired)
- ¾ cup crushed ice
- For the toppings
- (choose 1 or more)
- 2 to 3 raspberries, quartered
- 4 to 5 blueberries, quartered
- 2 strawberries cut into ¼-inch dice
- 2 slices peach cut into ¼-inch dice
- ½ tablespoon chia seeds

1. In a blender, combine all the ingredients. Process until the mixture is smooth and thick. Set aside any unoffered Purée before adding the toppings. Top with the your choice of cut raspberries, blueberries, strawberries, peach, and chia seeds.
2. The unoffered smoothie can be stored in the refrigerator for up to 3 days. Adjust the consistency with a little more ice to thicken it up and blend again before serving.

Banana and Avocado Superfood Smoothie

Julian's favorite Purée gets a smoothie makeover. Chia seeds and kale give his banana-avocado smoothie superfood status.

Prep time: 5 minutes | Cook time: 5 minutes|Serves 2 (1-cup)

- 6 ounces breast milk, formula, or any nondairy milk
- 2 tablespoons chia seeds
- 4 (1-ounce) freezer tray cubes kale purée, thawed
- ½ banana, peeled
- ½ avocado, pitted

1. In a blender, combine all the ingredients. Process until smooth. Store any unoffered smoothie in the refrigerator for up to 3 days.
2. When serving the remaining smoothie, adjust the consistency with a little extra liquid as needed and blend again before serving.

Strawberry and Cucumber Smoothie

Rich smoothies. In summer and early fall, I make this lighter version using fresh strawberries and cucumber.

Prep time: 5 minutes | Cook time: 5 minutes|Serves 2 (1-cup)

- 4 ounces breast milk, formula, or any nondairy milk
- ¼ cup plain yogurt
- ½ cup strawberries
- ½ Persian cucumber, unpeeled, cut into large chunks, or ½ English cucumber, seeds removed, cut into large chunks
- 1 to 2 medjool dates, pitted
- ¼ teaspoon minced, peeled fresh ginger

1. In a blender, combine all the ingredients. Process until smooth. Store any unoffered smoothie in the refrigerator for up to 3 days.
2. When serving the remaining smoothie, adjust the consistency with a little extra liquid as needed and blend again before serving.

Plum and Chard Smoothie

This smoothie helps ensure your baby gets lots of dark leafy greens as she gets older. Add 1 tablespoon nut butter, 1/4 cup yogurt, or 1/4 cup tofu for protein.

Prep time: 5 minutes | Cook time: 5 minutes|Serves 2 (1-cup)

- 6 ounces breast milk, formula, or any nondairy milk
- 3 (1-ounce) freezer tray cubes Swiss chard purée, thawed
- 3 (1-ounce) freezer tray cubes plum purée, thawed
- ¼ teaspoon ground ginger

1. In a blender, combine all the ingredients. Process until smooth. Store any unoffered smoothie in the refrigerator for up to 3 days.
2. When serving the remaining smoothie, adjust the consistency with a little extra liquid as needed and blend again before serving.

Orange Dream Smoothie

This orange smoothie provides protein, calcium, magnesium, fiber, and antioxidants for your baby's developing bones and muscles.

Prep time: 5 minutes | Cook time: 5 minutes|Serves 2 (1-cup)

- 6 ounces breast milk, formula, or any nondairy milk
- ¼ cup plain full-fat yogurt (nondairy if desired)
- 4 (1-ounce) freezer tray cubes sweet potato purée, thawed
- ¼ teaspoon ground ginger

1. In a blender, combine all the ingredients. Process until smooth. Store any unoffered smoothie in the refrigerator for up to 3 days.
2. When serving the remaining smoothie, adjust the consistency with a little extra liquid as needed and blend again before serving.

Broccoli Bites with Cottage Cheese and Chive Dip

The broccoli bits are soft and flavorful. Your baby will love dipping them in the calcium-rich cottage cheese dip. Wheat germ enhances any meal. It's rich in B vitamins, Vitamin E, zinc, and magnesium.

Prep time: 5 minutes | cook time: 15 minutes| Serves 4

FOR THE BROCCOLI BITES

- 1 cup broccoli florets
- 1 egg
- 1 tablespoon minced onion
- 1/3 cup grated Cheddar cheese
- ¼ cup wheat germ
- For the cottage cheese dip
- ¼ cup cottage cheese
- 2 tablespoons plain full-fat yogurt
- ¼ teaspoon onion powder
- ¼ teaspoon garlic powder
- 1 teaspoon chopped fresh chives
- To make the broccoli bites

1. Preheat the oven bto 400°F. Line a baking sheet with parchment.
2. In a small saucepan with a steamer insert, bring about 1 inch of water to a boil. Add the broccoli florets. Cover and steam for 1 minute. Chop the steamed broccoli into very small pieces.
3. Beat the egg in a small bowl. Add the broccoli, onion, cheese, and wheat germ. Mix well with a spoon.
4. Form the mixture into ½-inch balls. Place on the prepared baking sheet.
5. Bake for 20 minutes. Store unoffered broccoli bites in the refrigerator for up to 3 days or in the freezer for up to 6 months.

TO MAKE THE COTTAGE CHEESE DIP

In a blender or food processor, combine all the ingredients. Blend until smooth. Store unoffered portions in the refrigerator for up to 3 days.

Fruity Tofu Bites with Apple Yogurt Dip

This fruity snack is full of protein and calcium for growing babies. Cut tofu into small cubes your infant can handle and dunk.

Prep time: 5 minutes | Cook time: 15 minutes| Serves 4

- For the fruity tofu bites
- ¼ cup dried banana pieces
- ¼ teaspoon ground cinnamon
- ¼ cup almond flour
- 4 ounces extra firm tofu, cut into ½-inch cubes
- 1 egg, beaten
- For the apple yogurt dip
- 2 (1-ounce) freezer tray cubes apple Purée, thawed
- ¼ cup plain full-fat yogurt (nondairy if desired)
- ¼ teaspoon ground cinnamon
- To make the fruity tofu bites

1. Preheat the oven to 375°F. Line a baking sheet with parchment.
2. In a blender or food processor, process the bananas and cinnamon until they are finely ground. Transfer to a small bowl and stir in the almond flour.
3. Dip the pieces of tofu into the egg, and then coat each piece on all sides with the banana-almond flour mixture.
4. Arrange the coated tofu pieces on the prepared baking sheet and bake until the coating is golden brown, 10 to 15 minutes. Store any unoffered tofu bites in the refrigerator for up to 3 days or in the freezer for up to 6 months.

TO MAKE THE APPLE YOGURT DIP

In a blender or food processor, combine all the ingredients. Purée until smooth. Store unoffered portions in the refrigerator for up to 3 days.

Vanilla Butternut Squash Bites

Butternut squash tastes better with vanilla and nutmeg (or other winter squash, such as acorn). Baby will like the rich, caramelized flavor of roasted squash.

Prep time: 5 minutes | Cook time: 25 minutes| Serves 4

- 1 cup butternut squash, cut into ¼-inch dice
- 1 tablespoon olive oil
- ¼ teaspoon pure vanilla extract
- ¼ teaspoon ground nutmeg

1. Preheat the oven to 450°F. Line a baking sheet with parchment.
2. In a small bowl, toss the squash with the olive oil, vanilla, and nutmeg.
3. Place the squash in a single layer on the prepared baking sheet and bake, stirring once or twice, until browned, 15 to 20 minutes. Store any unoffered squash bites in the refrigerator for up to 3 days or in the freezer for up to 6 months.

Baked Apple Bites

Flaxseed and spices boost apples' health advantages. Flaxseed is high in fiber, which helps keep babies regular. High in omega-3 fatty acids, which reduce inflammation and assist the heart.

Prep time: 5 minutes | Cook time: 35 minutes| Serves 4

- ¼ cup flaxseed
- ¼ teaspoon ground cinnamon
- Pinch ground ginger
- 1 apple, peeled, cored, and cut into ½-inch pieces
- 1 egg, beaten

1. Preheat the oven to 375°F. Line a baking sheet with parchment.
2. In a blender or food processor, process the flaxseed, cinnamon, and ginger to make a powder. Transfer the powder to a small bowl.
3. Dip the pieces of apple into the egg, and then coat each piece on all sides with the flaxseed powder.
4. Arrange the pieces on the prepared baking sheet and bake until the apples are soft, 20 to 25 minutes. Store any unoffered baked apple in the refrigerator for up to 3 days or in the freezer for up to 6 months.

Pea Soup with Ham

Frozen peas make making soup easy. Breast milk, formula, water, broth, or yogurt can be used to modify the consistency.

Prep time: 5 minutes | Cook time: : 15 minutes| Serves 12 (2-ounce)

- 2 cups frozen peas
- 1 cup water or low-sodium chicken broth
- ¼ teaspoon onion powder
- ¼ teaspoon dried tarragon
- 3 ounces ham, finely diced

1. Put the peas, water, onion powder, and tarragon in a small pot. Bring to a simmer over medium-high heat, and cook until the peas are soft, about 5 minutes.
2. Transfer the mixture to a blender or food processor and purée. Add more water if desired to reach your needed consistency.
3. Return the purée to the pot and stir in the ham. Bring to a simmer, stirring, and heat through for about 3 minutes.
4. Cool slightly before serving.

Nut Butter and Banana Stackers

Meals aren't just meat and potatoes. There are near-infinite variations on nut butter "stackers." When you don't have time to cook, this is a lifesaver. Note: Nut butter foods should wait until baby is one and can swallow it.

Prep time: 5 minutes | Cook time: : 10 minutes| Serves 1

- 1 slice sprouted-wheat bread, crusts cut off
- 1 tablespoon nut butter (peanut, almond, etc.)
- ⅓ banana, sliced

1. Toast the bread slightly so it's still soft. Spread the nut butter on the bread.
2. Cut the bread into 1-inch squares.
3. Top each square with a banana slice and serve.

Ground Beef and Sweet Potato Soup

This soup is thinned with water or broth and sweet potato purée. Using the same pot to cook the beef and sweet potato adds flavor to the soup.

Prep time: 5 minutes | Cook time: : 25 minutes| Serves 12 (2-ounce servings)

- 2 teaspoons olive oil
- 4 ounces lean ground beef
- 1 sweet potato, peeled and cut into ½-inch pieces
- ½ teaspoon onion powder
- ½ teaspoon ground allspice
- ¾ cup water or low-sodium chicken broth

1. In a small pot over medium-high heat, heat the olive oil until it shimmers. Add the ground beef and cook, crumbling with a spatula, until it is well browned and in very small pieces, 5 to 7 minutes. Transfer the ground beef to a small bowl.
2. Add the sweet potato to the pot and cover with water to 1 inch above the potato. Cover and bring to a boil over high heat. Reduce the heat and simmer until the sweet potato is soft, about 15 minutes.
3. Drain the sweet potato, reserving about ½ cup of the cooking water. Combine the onion powder, allspice, and water or broth in a blender or food processor (or use an immersion blender right in the pot). Blend until smooth, adjusting the consistency with some of the reserved cooking water, if desired. Return the purée to the pot over medium heat.
4. Add the cooked ground beef. Simmer for 3 minutes, stirring constantly.
5. Cool slightly before serving.

Pasta with Veggies and White Beans

Whole-wheat pasta is a simple finger snack that's perfect for babies. I like to cut spaghetti into bite-size pieces and combine it with vegetables and legumes. If you don't want your toddler to get too messy, skip the smashed tomatoes in this recipe.

Prep time: 5 minutes | Cook time: : 15 minutes| Serves 8 (3-ounce)

- ½ cup dried whole-wheat or other whole-grain pasta (like penne)
- 1 cup (from 1 [16-ounce] package) frozen mixed vegetables (like carrots, peas, green beans, and corn)
- 1 teaspoon dried Italian seasoning
- ½ cup fresh or canned crushed tomatoes
- ½ cup canned white beans, rinsed and drained
- Grated Parmesan cheese (optional)

1. In a small pot of boiling water, cook the pasta until it is very soft. Drain, cool slightly, then cut into small pieces.
2. While the pasta is cooking, pour about ½ inch of water into another small pot fitted with a steamer basket, and add the mixed vegetables. Bring to a simmer over medium heat and steam until soft, 10 to 15 minutes.
3. In a medium skillet over medium-low heat, combine the cooked pasta, vegetables, Italian seasoning, tomatoes with their juices, and white beans, and heat until warmed through. Sprinkle with Parmesan cheese (if using), and serve warm.

Yam and Squash "Fries"

I often snacked on soft-cooked vegetables. Layla could easily pick up and eat these "fries" after experimenting with shapes and sizes. Serve with hummus or herb-flavored yogurt to entice kids. I prefer yams because of their deeper flavor and beta-carotene boost.

Prep time: 5 minutes | Cook time: : 15 minutes| Serves 4

- Olive oil spray
- 1 small yam, peeled and cut into ¼-inch matchsticks
- 1 zucchini or yellow squash, seeded and cut into ¼-inch matchsticks
- 1 tablespoon olive oil
- ¼ teaspoon garlic powder
- ¼ teaspoon paprika
- Several pinches kosher salt

1. Preheat the oven to 450°F. Coat a medium baking sheet with olive oil spray, or line it with parchment paper.
2. In a small bowl, combine the yam, zucchini, olive oil, garlic powder, paprika, and salt and toss to coat.
3. Spread the vegetable mixture on the prepared baking sheet in a single layer. Bake until the yam is lightly browned and fork-tender, 15 to 20 minutes.

Roasted Veggie Cubes

You can add any spice combination you like to these roasted vegetables. Roasted green beans and asparagus are delicious substitutes.

Prep time: 5 minutes | Cook time: : 15 minutes| Serves 4

- Olive oil spray
- 1 carrot, peeled and cut into ¼-inch cubes
- ½ medium butternut squash, peeled, seeded, and cut into ¼-inch cubes
- 1 beet, peeled and cut into ¼-inch cubes
- 1 tablespoon olive oil
- ½ teaspoon ground cumin
- ½ teaspoon ground coriander
- Pinch kosher salt

1. Preheat the oven to 450°F. Coat a medium baking sheet with olive oil spray, or line it with parchment paper.
2. In a small bowl, combine the carrot, butternut squash, beet, olive oil, cumin, coriander, and salt. Toss to coat.
3. Spread the mixture on the prepared baking sheet in a single layer. Bake until the vegetables are lightly browned and fork-tender, 15 to 20 minutes.

Tofu Nuggets

These tofu nuggets are a fun, mess-free snack. Whole-wheat flour adds fiber and complex carbs. Tip for dipping ideas.

Prep time: 5 minutes | Cook time: : 35 minutes| Serves 4

- 1 (16-ounce) package extra-firm tofu
- ¼ cup olive oil
- 1 cup whole-wheat flour, fine cornmeal, or oat flour
- ½ teaspoon garlic powder
- ½ teaspoon onion powder
- Pinch kosher salt

1. Preheat the oven to 400°F. Line a medium baking sheet with parchment paper.
2. Drain the tofu and press it with paper towels to get rid of as much excess water as possible. Cut it into 1-inch cubes.
3. Pour the olive oil into a small bowl. In a zip-top bag, combine the flour, garlic powder, onion powder, and salt. Take several tofu cubes, dunk them in the olive oil, then put them in the bag and shake to coat the tofu with the flour and spice mixture. Repeat with the remaining tofu.
4. Place the tofu nuggets on the prepared baking sheet. Bake for 15 minutes, flip the tofu nuggets, and bake for about 15 minutes more or until lightly browned and crispy on top.

Mini Banana-Blueberry Pancakes

Flourless pancakes are delicious. 1 tablespoon ground flaxseed boosts fiber and healthy fats. If you want to keep things simple, make banana pancakes with just bananas and eggs.

Prep time: 5 minutes | Cook time: 10 minutes| Serves about 8 (3-inch) pancakes

- ½ cup fresh or frozen blueberries
- 1 banana
- 2 eggs, beaten
- ¼ teaspoon ground cinnamon
- ¼ teaspoon ground nutmeg
- Olive oil spray

1. If you're using frozen blueberries, thaw them a little ahead of time, allowing the water or juices to drain off.
2. In a small bowl, mash the banana. Add the eggs, blueberries, cinnamon, and nutmeg and mix well.
3. Heat a griddle over medium heat and coat it with olive oil spray.
4. Pour about 2 tablespoons of batter for each pancake onto the griddle. Cook until bubbles form on top of the pancakes, 2 to 3 minutes. Flip and cook on the other side for another 2 to 3 minutes. Serve warm.

Healthy Oat Breakfast Cookies

These cookies contain nut butter, so they're best for "over-ones," but you can cut them into bite-size pieces for little hands. Make extra because they freeze well and make a healthy grab-and-go breakfast.

Prep time: 5 minutes | Cook time: : 15 minutes| Serves about 16 cookies

- Olive oil spray or 1 teaspoon olive oil
- 2 medium ripe bananas, mashed
- 2 tablespoons peanut butter (or any nut butter)
- 1 cup uncooked quick oats or rolled oats
- ¼ cup crushed walnuts
- ¼ teaspoon ground cinnamon

1. Preheat the oven to 350°F. Coat a medium nonstick baking sheet with olive oil spray or olive oil.
2. In a medium bowl, combine the mashed bananas and peanut butter. Add the oats and mix until thoroughly combined. Add the walnuts and cinnamon. Scoop 1 rounded tablespoon of batter onto the prepared baking sheet. Repeat with the remaining batter.
3. Bake for 15 minutes or until golden.

Pumpkin Mac and Cheese

This healthy cheese sauce tastes great over whole-wheat macaroni; pumpkin adds a rich, sweet flavor that pairs well with Cheddar. Broccoli gives this dish antioxidants and fiber.

Prep time: 5 minutes | Cook time:15 minutes| Serves 8 (½-cup)

- 1 medium pumpkin, peeled, seeded, and cut into 1-inch cubes
- ½ cup dried whole-wheat macaroni
- ¼ cup whole milk, plus more if needed
- ½ cup shredded Cheddar cheese
- ½ cup broccoli florets, steamed and cut into small pieces
- Salt
- Freshly ground black pepper

1. Pour about ½ inch of water into a medium pot and set a steamer basket inside it. Arrange the pumpkin evenly inside the basket. Bring the water to a simmer over medium heat and steam for 10 to 15 minutes, until the pumpkin is soft.
2. Meanwhile, cook the macaroni according to the package directions. Drain immediately.
3. Transfer the steamed pumpkin to a blender, add the milk and cheese, and purée until smooth. Add more milk to thin the sauce, if desired.
4. In a large bowl, combine the macaroni and broccoli with the pumpkin sauce, add salt and pepper to taste, and serve warm.

Orzo with Ground Turkey and Zucchini

Orzo is a great first solid food for toddlers. This "dry" recipe (no sauce) makes cleanup of your baby and her surroundings easy.

Prep time: 5 minutes | Cook time: : 15 minutes| Serves 6 (½-cup)

- 1 tablespoon olive oil
- 4 ounces ground turkey
- ¼ cup finely chopped onion
- 1 small zucchini, peeled and cut into ¼-inch cubes
- 1 garlic clove, minced
- 1 cup cooked orzo

1. In a small nonstick skillet over medium-high heat, heat the olive oil until it shimmers.
2. Add the ground turkey and cook, crumbling, until it is browned, about 5 minutes. Using a slotted spoon, remove the turkey and set aside on a plate.
3. Add the onion and zucchini to the skillet and cook, stirring occasionally, until the vegetables are soft, about 5 minutes.
4. Return the turkey to the skillet and add the garlic. Cook, stirring constantly, until the garlic is fragrant, about 30 seconds.
5. Toss in the orzo and cook to heat through, about 2 minutes.

Scrambled Egg Yolks with Veggies

Egg yolks are rarely allergenic, so this recipe uses only yolks. After a year, you can introduce egg whites and make this scramble with whole eggs.

Prep time: 5 minutes | Cook time: : 5 minutes| Serves 4

- 4 eggs
- 1 teaspoon olive oil
- 1 cup chopped cooked vegetables, like broccoli, bell peppers, spinach, or carrots
- ¼ teaspoon garlic powder
- ½ teaspoon dried oregano

1. Crack the eggs and separate the whites from the yolks. Reserve the whites for another use.
2. In a medium skillet over medium heat, warm the olive oil.
3. In a small bowl, beat the yolks. Add the vegetables, garlic powder, and oregano and stir to combine.
4. Pour the egg and vegetable mixture into the skillet.
5. Cook over medium heat, stirring constantly, until the yolks are scrambled and set. Let cool just slightly and serve.

Broccoli and Cheese Nuggets

These crispy-but-soft nuggets are great for little hands. Broccoli, cheese, eggs, and wheat germ (or oat flour) provide antioxidants, protein, and fiber, making this a complete mini-meal for your baby.

Prep time: 5 minutes | Cook time: : 25 minutes| Serves 8

- 2 eggs
- 1 (16-ounce) package frozen broccoli, steamed and chopped into very small pieces
- ½ cup wheat germ or oat flour
- ½ cup shredded Cheddar cheese
- 2 garlic cloves, minced

1. Preheat the oven to 400°F. Line a medium baking sheet with parchment paper.
2. In a small bowl, beat the eggs. Add the broccoli, wheat germ, cheese, and garlic. Mix well to combine.
3. Form the broccoli mixture into ½-inch balls. Place the balls on the prepared baking sheet.
4. Bake for about 20 minutes or until lightly browned and crispy on top.

Savory Sweet Potato, Lentil, and Carrot Cakes

These cakes are healthier versions of latkes, which are traditionally fried shredded-potato cakes. This recipe is a nutritional powerhouse for growing bodies thanks to the lentils and sweet potatoes.

Prep time: 5 minutes | Cook time: 15 minutes | Serves 8 cakes

- 1 cup peeled and shredded sweet potato
- 1 cup peeled and shredded carrot
- ½ cup cooked lentils, mashed
- 4 eggs
- 4 teaspoons whole-wheat flour, oat flour, or coconut flour
- Pinch kosher salt
- Olive oil spray

1. In a large bowl, combine the sweet potato, carrot, and lentils.
2. In a small bowl, whisk the eggs.
3. Add the flour to the sweet potato mixture, stirring to combine. Add the eggs and salt to the mixture and stir well.
4. Heat a large skillet over medium heat, and coat it with olive oil spray. Divide the sweet potato mixture into 8 parts, spooning each part onto the skillet. Flatten the cakes lightly with a spatula. Cook until the bottom is golden brown, about 5 minutes. Flip each cake and cook the other side until it is browned and crispy, another 5 minutes.
5. Cool before serving, cutting each cake into smaller pieces for bite-size chunks.

Rotini with Beef and Pumpkin Bolognese

Beef slow-cooked in dairy until tender and flavorful is typical of Bolognese. This quick, tasty version will delight your baby and you with vitamin A and protein.

Prep time: 5 minutes | Cook time: 15 minutes | Serves 6 (½-cup)

- 1 teaspoon olive oil
- 4 ounces ground beef
- ¼ cup finely chopped onion
- 1 garlic clove, minced
- 1 cup pumpkin purée or canned pumpkin purée
- ¼ cup water or low-sodium broth
- ¼ teaspoon ground sage
- ¾ cup rotini, cooked according to package directions and drained

1. In a small pot over medium-high heat, heat the olive oil until it shimmers. Add the ground beef and cook, stirring and crumbling, until browned, 5 to 7 minutes.
2. Add the onion and cook, stirring occasionally, until the onion is soft, 3 to 5 minutes more.
3. Add the garlic and cook, stirring constantly, for 30 seconds.
4. Add the pumpkin purée, then add the water 1 tablespoon at a time until you achieve your desired consistency. Stir in the sage and simmer for about 2 minutes more.
5. 5.Add the rotini and heat through.

Salmon and Sweet Potato Cakes

The recipe calls for salmon, but any pink-fleshed fish will do. Remove all pinbones from the fish and flake it into small pieces so your baby can chew it.

Prep time: 5 minutes | Cook time: 35 minutes | Serves 12 cakes

- 4 ounces salmon
- ½ sweet potato, peeled and cut into 1-inch cubes
- ½ teaspoon chopped fresh dill
- ¼ teaspoon onion powder
- 1 egg, lightly beaten
- 2 tablespoons olive oil

1. In a small saucepan, bring about 1 cup of water to a simmer, and poach the salmon for 7 to 10 minutes. Remove the salmon from the water and allow it to cool a bit. Remove the skin and any pinbones, then flake the fish with a fork.
2. In a small pot, cover the sweet potato with water and bring to a boil. Boil until the potato is soft, about 10 minutes.
3. Transfer the potato to a medium bowl and mash. Add the dill and onion powder.
4. Stir in the egg and the poached salmon. Mix until well combined.
5. In a large nonstick skillet over medium-high heat, heat the olive oil until it shimmers.
6. Form the potato-salmon mixture into 12 balls, then flatten them and place in the skillet. Cook in the hot oil until browned on both sides, about 5 minutes per side.

Chicken and White Bean Fritters

White beans bind these chicken fritters. These tasty treats are a good source of protein and carbs for small and large fingers.

Prep time: 5 minutes | Cook time: 15 minutes | Serves 12 fritters

- 1 teaspoon olive oil, plus 2 tablespoons used later
- 1 medium carrot, peeled and grated
- 1 cup canned white beans, rinsed and drained
- ¼ teaspoon dried thyme
- ¼ teaspoon garlic powder
- 4 ounces ground chicken, browned and drained

1. In a small sauté pan or skillet over medium-high heat, heat 1 teaspoon of olive oil until it shimmers. Add the carrot and cook, stirring occasionally, until soft, about 5 minutes. Allow to cool completely.
2. Transfer the carrot to a blender or food processor. Add the beans, thyme, and garlic powder and purée.
3. Transfer the purée to a medium bowl and stir in the cooked chicken. Form the mixture into 12 small balls. Press the balls flat into patties.
4. In a large nonstick skillet over medium-high heat, heat the remaining 2 tablespoons of olive oil until it shimmers.
5. Place the patties in the skillet and cook until browned on both sides, about 4 minutes per side.
6. Cool slightly before serving.

Chapter 6
Toddler Meals(12-18 Months)

The time has come for baby to sit and enjoys its meals with the family. It is important to note that you should prepare the baby's food in a similar way to the family's have but it should be softer for the baby to chew. You should have readily available homemade meals as they are healthier than processed food. You could prepare something like a vegetable dip or toast fingers. Unlike adults, kids can't eat much food at once but will eat in bits so it is important as a parent to understand this and feed your child accordingly. Children learn through experiments. Its sense of adventure is growing as the changes are occur. Therefore, you should let them sit at the table and learn from the rest of the family.

Some foods recommended at this stage include turkey nuggets, egg mayonnaise sandwiches, and pork and apple sausage rolls. You will find recipes in this book to help you prepare that nice meal you've always wanted to prepare for your baby. Unlike other stages where you prioritize breast milk or formula, solid food comes first at this stage. You may decide to stop breastfeeding, but it is advisable to continue until the baby reaches two years of age. Provide your baby with foods that meet their appetite and tastes as this will provide for their nutritional needs. Do not forget a glass of milk or water to help with hydration.

Coconut Lentil Stew

This satisfying recipe would also be delicious with unsalted butter instead of coconut oil as the cooking fat.

Prep time: 5 minutes | Cook time: 35 minutes| Serves 3

- 1 tablespoon plus 1 teaspoon coconut oil
- ½ cup finely chopped yellow onion
- 1 teaspoon cumin
- ½ teaspoon ground coriander
- ½ teaspoon turmeric
- 3 cups low-sodium chicken broth
- 1 cup red lentils, rinsed
- ½ teaspoon salt, or more to taste

1. Heat 1 tablespoon of coconut oil in a medium saucepan over medium-low heat. Add the onion and sauté until lightly browned, 8 to 10 minutes.
2. Add the cumin, coriander, and turmeric. Stir to coat the onion and cook for 2 minutes.
3. Add the chicken broth and bring to a boil. Add the lentils and salt. Reduce the heat to medium-low, partially cover, and simmer until the lentils are tender, about 20 minutes. The lentils should be thick, not soupy. If you find that they are becoming too thick, cover the pan for the final minutes of cooking.

Stuffed Sweet Potatoes

This recipe takes about 20 minutes, although only 10 are active. If you're in a hurry, pierce the sweet potatoes and microwave them on high for 6 to 8 minutes. You'll miss the caramelization from roasting, but there's no shame in a shortcut.

Prep time: 5 minutes | Cook time: 15 minutes| Serves 2

- 2 medium sweet potatoes (about 1 pound)
- ½ cup canned pinto beans, drained and rinsed
- 2 teaspoons mild salsa, plus more for topping
- ¼ cup shredded cheddar cheese

1. Preheat the oven to 425°F. Line a rimmed baking sheet with parchment paper or aluminum foil. Place the sweet potatoes on the baking sheet and roast until completely tender, about 35 minutes. Let cool for 5 to 10 minutes.
2. In a small microwave-safe bowl, stir together the beans and salsa. Heat in the microwave for 15 seconds.
3. Slice open the top of the sweet potatoes and open them up so they are mostly flat. Serve at the table with the cheese, bean and salsa mixture, and more salsa for topping.

E.A.T. Sandwich

My daughter and I adore BLTs, but the E.A.T. is much better and healthier. When tomatoes are in season, eat this sandwich. Since the ingredients are basic, salt it well.

Prep time: 5 minutes | Cook time: 5 minutes | Makes 2 sandwiches

- 4 slices whole-wheat bread, toasted
- ½ avocado, mashed
- salt
- 2 teaspoons olive oil
- 2 eggs
- freshly ground pepper, to taste
- 2 slices tomato

1. Using a 3-inch round cookie cutter, cut a large circle out of each piece of toast. Divide the mashed avocado evenly between 2 circles. Sprinkle with salt.
2. Heat the olive oil in a medium skillet over medium heat. Crack the eggs into the skillet and sprinkle with salt and pepper. Cover the pan and cook until the yolks are mostly cooked through, about 3 minutes. Flip the eggs with a spatula and remove the pan from the heat. Transfer the eggs to a cutting board and use the cookie cutter to shape them into circles. Place an egg circle on each slice of avocado-smeared toast.
3. Top the eggs with the tomato slices. Sprinkle with salt and cover with the remaining toast circles.

Curried Chicken Salad in Mini Pitas

This recipe uses leftover chicken. Poaching a chicken breast takes 15 minutes in barely boiling water.

Prep time: 5 minutes | Cook time: 5 minutes| Makes 3 sandwiches

- 2 tablespoons plain greek yogurt
- 2 tablespoons mayonnaise
- 1 tablespoon white wine vinegar
- 1 teaspoon curry powder
- ½ teaspoon turmeric
- ½ teaspoon salt
- 1 cooked chicken breast, shredded (about 1¼ cups meat)
- ¼ cup finely chopped celery
- 3 tablespoons raisins
- 2 tablespoons chopped cilantro
- 3 mini pitas, top ½-inch cut off

1. In a medium bowl, stir together the yogurt, mayonnaise, vinegar, curry powder, turmeric, and salt. Add the chicken breast, celery, and raisins and toss to coat. Stir in the cilantro.
2. Divide the chicken between the pitas and serve.

Tortellini Soup

Tortellini soup is toddler catnip, in my experience (and bigger kids). This dish comes together quickly with a well-stocked pantry. Frozen vegetables can replace broccoli; cook according to package instructions. Dried tortellini are smaller than fresh or frozen. Pasta aisle.

Prep time: 5 minutes | Cook time: 15 minutes| Serves 2

3 cups low-sodium chicken broth
4 oz. dried cheese-filled tortellini
2 cups small broccoli florets (about ½ bunch)
⅛ teaspoon salt
½ teaspoon lemon juice
freshly ground pepper, to taste
grated parmesan cheese (optional)

1. In a medium saucepan, bring the broth to a boil. Add the tortellini and cook for 5 minutes.
2. Add the broccoli and cook for 5 minutes more or until the tortellini and the broccoli are tender. Add the salt and lemon juice. Pour into 2 serving bowls and garnish with pepper and Parmesan to taste.

20-Minute Mac 'n' Cheese

Mac-and-cheese in under 30 minutes? Certainly. This creamy mac is better than boxed and healthier. (Check the box's ingredients.)

Prep time: 5 minutes | Cook time: 25 minutes| Serves 4

- salt
- 2 cups multi-grain elbow macaroni (8 oz.)
- 2 tablespoons unsalted butter
- 2 tablespoons flour
- 1½ cups milk
- ½ teaspoon dijon mustard
- 1½ cups shredded sharp cheddar cheese (4 oz.)
- freshly ground pepper, to taste

1. Bring a medium pot of salted water to a boil. Cook the macaroni according to package directions. Drain and return to the pot.
2. Meanwhile, melt the butter in a small saucepan over medium heat. Add the flour and whisk until smooth and bubbly. Cook for 2 minutes or until the mixture is a light tan.
3. Whisk in the milk. Bring to a simmer, whisking frequently to remove any lumps. Whisk in the mustard and ½ teaspoon salt. Simmer for 5 minutes, stirring occasionally. Remove the sauce from the heat and stir in the cheese until fully melted.
4. Pour the cheese sauce over the pasta. Stir to combine, and add freshly ground pepper to taste.

Crispy Quesadillas

I'd eat a freshly prepared quesadilla with these healthful components any day of the week. Variate the filling to use up leftovers. Think shredded meat, broccoli, or apples.

Prep time: 5 minutes | Cook time: 5 minutes| Serves 2

- ½ cup canned low-sodium black beans, drained and rinsed
- 1 tablespoon plain greek yogurt
- two 8-inch flour tortillas
- ⅛ teaspoon salt
- ¼ cup butternut squash purée
- ¼ cup shredded sharp cheddar cheese
- 2 teaspoons canola oil

1. In a small bowl, mash the beans with a fork. Stir in the yogurt. Using the back of a spoon or a knife, divide the bean mixture between the two tortillas, leaving a 1-inch border around the edges. Sprinkle each with a pinch of salt.
2. In another small bowl, stir together the butternut squash purée and the shredded cheese. Spread over one half of one tortilla on top of the beans, continuing to leave a 1-inch border. Fold the tortilla over to make a half-moon. Repeat with the second tortilla.
3. Heat the canola oil in a small skillet over medium heat. Add one quesadilla to the pan and cook until it is golden brown and the cheese is melted, about 2 minutes per side. Repeat with the second quesadilla. Cut into wedges and serve.

Quinoa Bowl

Quinoa is a rice substitute and salad ingredient. Quinoa in a parfait may be a first. This recipe completes your yogurt parfait. Family members can design their own bowls with this deconstructed snack.

Prep time: 5 minutes | Cook time: 5 minutes| Serves 3

- 1 cup cooked quinoa
- 1 cup milk or full-fat plain Greek yogurt (yogurt or milk alternative for vegan option)
- 1 cup berries
- ¼ cup toppings (shelled hemp seeds, sunflower seeds, finely chopped nuts, shredded coconut)

1. Separate the ingredients into serving bowls and place them on the table with serving spoons.
2. Have each family member build a bowl, using quinoa as a base.

Morning Glory Muffins

My family loves muffins. Nutritious, freezeable, and thaw quickly. These muffins are terrific snacks for small hands. Double the recipe and freeze for busy days. This dough is thick because the carrots and apples shed moisture while they bake, like Chocolate Bloomies.

Prep time: 5 minutes | Cook time: 35 minutes| Serves 18

- Nonstick cooking spray (optional)
- 1½ cups whole-wheat flour
- ½ cup all-purpose flour
- ¾ cup brown sugar
- 1 tablespoon baking powder
- 2 teaspoons baking soda
- 2 teaspoons cinnamon
- ½ teaspoon salt
- 1 tablespoon vanilla extract
- 2 cups carrot, grated
- ½ cup raisins

1. Preheat the oven to 375°F.
2. Prepare two 12-cup muffin tins with paper or silicone liners or grease the pan with the nonstick cooking spray, if using.
3. Mix the flours, sugar, baking powder, baking soda, cinnamon, and salt in a large mixing bowl.
4. In a medium-size mixing bowl, combine the applesauce, oil, apple, and vanilla.
5. Pour the wet ingredients into the dry ingredients and mix until just combined.
6. Fold in the carrots and raisins.
7. Fill each muffin cup to two-thirds full and bake for 25 to 28 minutes, or until golden.

Plantain Tostones

The simplest dishes are often the best. Tostones are a popular Caribbean and Latin American street meal. Half-inch portions are perfect for little hands. These must be double-fried. First-fry plantain releases starches but doesn't soften texture. The second, hotter fry softens the inside and crisps the outside. Hot or cold, tostones are delicious.

Prep time: 5 minutes | Cook time: 15 minutes| Serves 3

- 2 green plantains
- ¼ cup rice flour
- ½ cup cooking oil, like avocado oil
- Sea salt

1. Peel the plantains. Slice off the top and bottom of the plantain with a sharp knife. Slice lengthwise through the tough outer skin in three places. Peel the skin from the plantain to expose the starchy fruit. Discard the skins.
2. Slice the plantains into discs about ½ inch thick.
   Dust each disc in rice flour.
3. Heat the oil in a nonstick skillet on medium heat. Fry the plantains for 2 to 3 minutes on each side. Drain excess oil on a kitchen towel.
4. Place the fried plantain discs on a sheet of parchment paper. Sprinkle them with rice flour, then cover with another sheet of parchment paper. Roll or mash the plantains gently between the parchment paper.
5. Increase the temperature for the skillet to medium-high heat. Fry the plantains for 2 to 3 minutes on each side, until golden brown.
6. Drain on a kitchen towel and sprinkle immediately with sea salt.

Dipped Banana and Chia Jam Sandwich

These are terrific snacks or sides. The banana sweetens their tartness. Once you master chia jam, explore different tastes. I like it with berries and lemon, but the possibilities are unlimited. Use leftover chia jam for PB&J Sandwich Kabobs, French Toast Sticks, or cereal.

Prep time: 5 minutes | Cook time: 45 minutes| Makes 5 sandwiches

- 1 pound fresh strawberries, (or frozen and thawed), hulled and roughly chopped
- 3 tablespoons honey or maple syrup
- 1 teaspoon lemon juice
- 2 tablespoons chia seeds
- 1 banana
- ½ cup plain full-fat Greek yogurt (yogurt alternative for vegan option)

1. In a medium pot over medium heat, boil the chopped strawberries and honey. The strawberries will release moisture and then begin to boil.
2. As bubbles begin to form, remove from heat and use a metal fork or a potato masher to carefully mash the hot strawberries.
3. Mix in the lemon juice and the chia seeds, then let the mixture sit, uncovered, to cool.
4. When the chia jam has reached room temperature to slightly warm, peel the banana and slice it into 10 slices.
5. Prepare a baking sheet by lining it with parchment paper or foil. Place the banana slices on the prepared baking sheet.
6. Cover a banana slice with some chia jam, then top it with another banana slice to make a sandwich.
7. Make 5 sandwiches, then set aside the remaining chia jam.
8. Freeze the sandwiches for 45 to 60 minutes.
9. Take the sandwiches out of the freezer and dip them, either half or whole, in the yogurt. Place them back on the pan and freeze for at least an hour.
10. Enjoy!

Frozn Yogurt Bark

Yogurt has health benefits. Fat promotes brain growth. Probiotics improve gut health. Greek yogurt provides more calcium and protein than conventional yogurt. So versatile! Even toddlers can assist make this colorful snack or dessert. Let your child help top yogurt with toppings.

Prep time: 5 minutes | Cook time: 5 minutes| Serves 5

- 2 cups full-fat Greek yogurt (yogurt alternative for vegan option)
- 2 tablespoons maple syrup
- ½ teaspoon vanilla extract
- ½ cup toppings (sliced strawberries, blueberries, shredded coconut, dark chocolate shavings, finely chopped dried cranberries or raisins, crushed nuts, hulled hemp seeds, ½ teaspoon lemon zest)

1. Mix the yogurt, maple syrup, and vanilla extract in a small mixing bowl.
2. Line a baking tray with wax paper.
3. Pour the yogurt mix onto the prepared baking tray and spread it evenly, ideally not thicker than ½ inch at any point.
4. Sprinkle the toppings over the yogurt.
5. Place in the freezer for 2 to 4 hours, until hard, then use a sharp knife to break the bark into pieces. Enjoy!

Sweet Potato Waffles

Sweet waffles without syrup? Okay. Not overmixing the batter makes light waffles. Overmixing creates a dense, hard waffle. While the waffle iron warms, let the batter rest for 5 minutes. Waffles expand in the iron, so use less batter.

Prep time: 5 minutes | Cook time: 35 minutes| Makes 11 to 12 waffles

2 cups all-purpose flour (gluten-free flour optional)
¼ teaspoon sea salt
1 tablespoon double-acting baking powder
3 large eggs (flax eggs for vegan option)
½ cup milk (milk alternative for vegan option)
½ cup buttermilk (buttermilk alternative for vegan option)
½ cup melted butter (butter alternative for vegan option)
1 teaspoon vanilla extract
1 tablespoon maple syrup
1 cup sweet potato purée

1. Combine the flour, salt, and baking powder in a small bowl and whisk to mix.
2. In a large bowl, whisk the eggs. Add the milk and buttermilk and whisk. Add the melted butter and mix well. Add the vanilla, maple syrup, and sweet potato, mixing well.
3. Add the flour mixture to the wet ingredients, folding gently to incorporate, making sure not to overmix.
4. Let the batter rest for 5 minutes to activate the baking powder.
5. Preheat the waffle iron.
6. Spoon the batter into the preheated waffle iron.
7. Cook for 5 to 7 minutes according to your waffle iron instructions.

Kedgeree with Flaked Whitefish

This tasty breakfast dish also makes a great lunch or dinner. Rice softens and tastes enhance when simmered in flavored cream.

Prep time: 5 minutes | Cook time: 45 minutes| Serves 4 (1-cup)

- 1 cup long grain rice
- 1½ cups water
- 4 large eggs
- 2 tablespoons olive oil
- ½ Vidalia onion, diced
- 2 garlic cloves, minced
- 1 tablespoon curry powder
- 2 teaspoons salt
- 1 cup heavy cream
- 2½ pounds whitefish, like smoked haddock
- 1 bay leaf
- 1 tablespoon lemon juice
- ½ cup minced flat leaf parsley

1. Rinse the rice under cold water until the water runs clear. Pour 1½ cups of water into a pot and add the rice. Bring to a boil, then reduce heat to low, cooking for 10 minutes. Check for doneness (see tip), then drain and discard any remaining cooking water. Set the rice aside.
2. In the same pot, bring salted water to a boil and cook the eggs for 10 minutes. When the eggs are finished cooking, immerse them immediately in ice water to stop them from cooking further.
3. When the eggs are cool, peel and chop them, then set aside.
4. Heat the olive oil on medium in a clean pot. When the oil shimmers and quickly coats the bottom, add the onion and garlic and sauté until translucent, careful to avoid burning. Add the curry powder and sauté for 1 minute. Add the salt, heavy cream, fish, and bay leaf.
5. Bring to a simmer. Remove the bay leaf, add the rice and lemon juice, and mix to coat with sauce. Cook for 5 minutes.
6. Remove the pot from the heat and add the parsley and chopped eggs. Gently fold to mix.

Cornbread with Scrambled Eggs

Scrambled eggs and skillet corn bread are a delicious combination. This recipe bakes best in a cast iron skillet, but a loaf or pie pan works too. Traditional southern cornbread is sweetened by sweet yellow cornmeal, so no sugar is needed. Eggs and cornbread are wonderful for baby-led weaning. See here for homemade buttermilk.

Prep time: 5 minutes | Cook time: 15 minutes| Serves 3

- For the cornbread
- 2½ cups yellow cornmeal
- 1 cup all-purpose flour (gluten-free flour optional)
- 2 teaspoons salt
- 1 teaspoon baking powder
- 1 teaspoon baking soda
- 2 large eggs
- 1 cup milk
- 1¾ cups buttermilk
- 2 tablespoons melted butter
- For the scrambled eggs
- 4 large eggs
- ¼ cup milk
- Pinch salt
- Pinch pepper
- 2 teaspoons butter
- To make the cornbread

1. Preheat a cast iron skillet in the oven at 375°F.
2. In a mixing bowl, whisk together the cornmeal, flour, salt, baking powder, and baking soda.
3. In a separate bowl, whisk together the eggs, milk, buttermilk, and melted butter.
4. Add the dry ingredients to the wet ingredients, then fold to incorporate.
5. Add the batter to the hot skillet, smoothing the top with a spatula. Bake for 35 minutes, or until a toothpick inserted in the center comes out clean.
6. Cool in the pan on a wire rack. Slice and serve hot.
7. make the scrambled eggs
8. In a medium-size mixing bowl, beat the eggs, milk, salt, and pepper.
9. Heat the butter in a large pan over medium heat until it just begins to brown.
10. Pour the egg mixture into the pan. As the eggs begin to set, use a spatula to pull them apart and form large, soft pieces.
11. Continue cooking by pulling, lifting, and folding the eggs until no liquid egg remains.
12. Serve after cooling to warm.

Egg and Cheese Breakfast Quesadilla

In terms of complexity, this quesadilla couldn't be easier to make. The quesadillas are excellent for re-heating on a hectic morning and may be frozen for later use.

Prep time: 5 minutes | Cook time: 5 minutes| Makes 4 quesadillas

- 2 tablespoons butter, divided into 4 equal pieces
- 4 large eggs
- 8 corn tortillas, warmed
- 2 cups shredded Mexican cheese

1. In a skillet over medium heat, melt 1 piece of butter. Crack 1 egg into the skillet. Use a spatula to break the yolk, cook for 1 minute, then flip. Cook on the other side for 1 minute. Remove from the skillet and set aside. Repeat with remaining eggs.
2. Place 1 warmed tortilla to cook in the same skillet.
3. Top the tortilla with shredded cheese. Add a cooked egg and top with more cheese. Top with a second tortilla.
4. Cover and let cook for 1 minute.
5. Flip and cook covered on the other side for 1 minute.
6. Repeat steps 2 through 5 the with remaining tortillas.
7. Cut each quesadilla in half, then in half again. Serve hot with your favorite salsa.

Acai Fruit Bowl

This naturally sweet recipe is a delicious breakfast or hot-day treat. These bowls, inspired by a trip to Brazil, are a refreshing summertime treat. Freeze banana slices for simple fruit bowls. This dish uses acai juice or purée. The juice is more widely available, while the purée is in some supermarket freezers. Alternatively, you can use pomegranate juice. This recipe helps sore throats and teething babies.

Prep time: 5 minutes | Cook time: 5 minutes| Serves 2 (1-cup)

- 8 ounces acai juice
- 1 banana, diced into chunks, frozen
- ½ cup pitted cherries, frozen
- Toppings of choice

1. Combine the acai juice, banana, and cherries in a blender.
2. Blend until smooth.
3. Add toppings of choice such as frozen berries, granola, almond slivers, or diced chocolate.

Crepes with Hazelnut Spread

French crepes are light pancakes. Prepare butter portions and a batter measuring cup. A quick wrist flick thins the batter. I use a 10-inch shallow skillet and a silicone spatula to make crepes. Serve as a brunch or afternoon snack. Savory crepes, anyone? Substitute meats, cheeses, or eggs for vanilla. Justin's Chocolate Hazelnut and Almond Butter is my fave.

Prep time: 5 minutes | Cook time: 5 minutes | Makes 8 crepes

- ¼ cup milk
- 3 large eggs
- 1 teaspoon vanilla extract
- ½ cup tapioca flour
- Pinch salt
- 4 tablespoons butter, divided into 8 pieces
- 1 jar hazelnut spread, warmed
- 1 cup strawberries, hulled and thinly sliced

1. In a small bowl, whisk the milk with the eggs until smooth. Add the vanilla and whisk to mix.
2. In a medium bowl, mix the tapioca flour and salt.
3. Add the wet ingredients to the dry mixture and stir gently to mix. The batter will be runny.
4. Heat 1 piece of butter in a 10-inch nonstick skillet over medium heat.
5. Add ¼ cup of batter to the pan and swirl to coat. Cook for 30 to 50 seconds.
6. Gently flip the crepe with a spatula and cook for 30 to 50 seconds more.
7. Place the crepe on a kitchen towel and cover to keep warm as you cook the remaining crepes.
8. To serve, spread the warmed hazelnut spread across the crepe. Top with the strawberries.

Flatbread Pizza

Pizza lovers unite! Flatbread pizza is a quick dinner or do-it-yourself celebration. Pizza is an excellent way to introduce your toddler to colorful vegetables. Build a masterpiece with lavash, tortillas, or matzo.

Prep time: 5 minutes | Cook time: 25 minutes | Serves 4

- Vegetables for topping, such as spinach, bell peppers, mushrooms, cherry tomatoes (halved lengthwise)
- Olive oil spray (optional)
- 1 flatbread (gluten-free flatbread optional)
- 3 tablespoons marinara sauce, veggieful Sauce, or pesto
- 2 ounces shredded mozzarella cheese (cheese alternative for vegan option)
- ¼ teaspoon Italian seasoning

1. Preheat the oven to 450°F.
2. Chop the vegetables for topping and set aside.
3. Prepare a baking sheet by spraying it with oil or lining it with a sheet of parchment paper. Lay out the flatbread on the prepared pan.
4. Spread the sauce on the flatbread with a spoon, being careful not to add too much, or the flatbread will become soggy.
5. Add the vegetables and sprinkle the cheese and Italian seasoning on top.
6. Bake until the cheese is melted and starts to brown, 10 to 15 minutes.
7. Let cool, slice, and enjoy!

Shrimp and Avocado Salad

Kids love superfood avocado. Healthy omega-3 fatty acids are supplied in a way youngsters would eat. Together with the shrimp, this recipe delivers vital protein for a nutritious family supper.

Prep time: 10 minutes | Cook time: 6 minutes| Serves 4

- 3 tablespoons extra-virgin olive oil
- 2 garlic cloves, minced
- 1 teaspoon minced fresh parsley
- 1 pound raw shrimp
- ½ teaspoon sweet paprika
- Pinch sea salt
- 4 Hass avocados, peeled, pitted, and diced, shells reserved
- ½ cup frozen corn, thawed

1. In a medium skillet over medium-high heat, warm the olive oil. Add the garlic and parsley and cook for 2 minutes. Add the shrimp, paprika, and salt and cook until they turn pink, about 4 minutes. Be careful not to overcook them. Turn off the heat and let the shrimp cool.
2. Add the avocado and corn and stir to combine.
3. To make it more toddler-friendly: Cut the cooked shrimp into toddler-size bites and mash the avocado with a fork.
4. Spoon the salad into the avocado shells and serve.

Tuna Panzanella

Panzanella combines bread with tomatoes. Please add anything else. Extra-virgin olive oil-packed tuna tastes finest. The soft, spongy bread in this salad is great for small mouths. Start this dish a day ahead so the bread may dry out.

Prep time: 20 minutes| Serves 6

- 1½ baguettes, cut into 1-inch pieces
- 1½ cups quartered cherry tomatoes
- 5 tablespoons extra-virgin olive oil, divided
- ½ teaspoon sea salt
- 2 cups water
- 2 tablespoons apple cider vinegar
- 10 ounces canned tuna in extra-virgin olive oil
- 1 cup frozen corn, thawed
- 1 Hass avocado, peeled, pitted, and diced
- 1 Persian cucumber, diced
- ½ cup sweet green olives, pitted and minced
- 5 fresh basil leaves
- 2 tablespoons soy sauce
- 1 lemon, cut into quarters and very thinly sliced

1. The day before you want to serve the salad, place the baguette pieces in a large bowl and leave them on the kitchen counter to dry out.
2. In a medium bowl, mix together the tomatoes, 3 tablespoons olive oil, and the salt. Set aside.
3. In a measuring cup, mix together the water with the vinegar and pour it over the dried bread. Let sit for 5 minutes.
4. Add the tuna, corn, avocado, cucumber, olives, basil, soy sauce, lemon, and the remaining 2 tablespoons olive oil and mix until combined. Add the tomatoes, stir to combine, and serve.

Cauliflower and Fish Croquettes

Cauliflower transforms this dish. It offers croquettes nourishment, body, and moisture. For a lighter option, I prefer to bake them. Almond meal coating is nutty.

Prep time: 15 minutes | Cook time: 30 minutes| Serves 6

- 1½ cups water
- ½ pound cauliflower, cut into pieces
- 1 pound catfish fillet, cut into big pieces
- 3 tablespoons almond meal, plus 1 cup for coating
- 1 tablespoon parsley, minced
- 1 teaspoon garlic powder
- 1 egg
- ½ teaspoon sea salt
- ¼ cup extra-virgin olive oil

1. In a large pot over medium-high heat, bring the water to a boil. Add the cauliflower, cover, then reduce the heat to medium-low. Cook until tender, 8 to 10 minutes.
2. Preheat the oven to 400°F. Line a baking sheet with parchment paper.
3. In a food processor, pulse the catfish for a few seconds until finely minced. Add the steamed cauliflower and pulse for a few seconds to combine the ingredients. Transfer to a large bowl and mix together with 3 tablespoons almond meal, the parsley, garlic, egg, and salt.
4. Using your hands, form small croquettes with 1 tablespoon of the mixture for each one. If the mixture is too sticky, wet your hands with water.
5. Pour 1 cup almond meal in a small bowl. Dredge each croquette in the almond meal, making sure to cover it all over.
6. Place the croquettes onto the prepared baking sheet and drizzle with the olive oil. Bake for 20 minutes, until heated through.

Salmon and Broccoli Fusilli

Salmon is high in brain-healthy fats and low in mercury, so I feed it to my kids at least once a week. This dish will satisfy anyone bored with plain roasted salmon or wary of fish.

Prep time: 15 minutes | Cook time: 13 minutes| Serves 6

- 1 pound fusilli pasta
- 3 tablespoons extra-virgin olive oil, divided
- ½ medium white onion, minced
- 4 garlic cloves, minced
- 1 head broccoli, stems discarded, florets cut into small pieces
- ¼ cup warm water
- Pinch sea salt
- 8 ounces salmon, diced
- 1 tablespoon minced fresh parsley
- 3 tablespoons plain yogurt

1. Bring a large pot of water to a boil, add the pasta, and cook according to the package instructions. Drain the pasta, reserving 1 cup of the pasta water. Set aside.
2. In a large sauté pan or skillet over medium-high heat, warm 2 tablespoons olive oil. Add the onion and garlic and cook for 3 minutes. Reduce the heat to medium-low, add the broccoli florets, parsley, warm water, and salt and cook for 8 minutes. Transfer the broccoli to a bowl and set aside.
3. To make it more toddler-friendly: Process the cooked broccoli in a food processor until smooth and set aside.
4. In the same skillet over medium heat, add the remaining 1 tablespoon olive oil, the salmon, and salt and cook for 2 minutes, stirring occasionally.
5. Add the broccoli back to the skillet and stir. Remove from the heat.
6. Add the pasta and yogurt to the salmon mixture and stir to combine. If the sauce is too thick, add the reserved pasta water, 1 tablespoon at a time, until you reach the desired consistency. Serve warm, or cooled to room temperature for toddlers.

Cod and Zucchini Shells Pasta

Seafood, vegetables, and pasta form a fantastic family feast. All the ingredients are diced into bite-size pieces, so the cod and zucchini sauce naturally fills the pasta shells. Anchovies replace salt and provide omega-3 fatty acids for your toddler's brain.

Prep time: 20 minutes | Cook time: 20 minutes| Serves 4

- 1 pound shell pasta or any short pasta
- 1 tablespoon sea salt
- 4 tablespoons extra-virgin olive oil, divided
- 2 anchovy fillets or ½ teaspoon sea salt
- 2 garlic cloves, minced
- 2 zucchinis, quartered and cut into thick slices
- 1 heirloom tomato, seeds removed and diced
- ½ pound cod, diced
- 1 tablespoon minced fresh parsley
- 2 tablespoons almond meal
- 2 tablespoons bread crumbs
- Parmesan cheese, for serving

1. Bring a pot of water to a boil over high heat, add the pasta and salt, and cook according to the package instructions. Drain the pasta, reserving 1 cup of the pasta water. Set aside.
2. In a large sauté pan or skillet over medium heat, warm 2 tablespoons olive oil. Add the anchovies and garlic and cook for 2 minutes. Add the zucchinis and cook for an additional 4 minutes. Add the tomatoes, cod, and parsley, then stir and cook for 5 minutes. Transfer the mixture to a large bowl and set aside.
3. In the same skillet over medium heat, stir together the almond meal and breadcrumbs until they start to brown, about 2 minutes.
4. Add the pasta to the large bowl with the cod and stir to combine. Add the breadcrumb mixture and the remaining 2 tablespoons olive oil and stir gently to combine. Serve warm.
5. To make it more toddler-friendly: Cool to room temperature and add a generous handful of grated Parmesan cheese on top.

Skillet Mahi-Mahi with Pesto, Tomatoes, and Olives

I used to make this using chicken. I ran out of chicken and substituted mahi-mahi. Fish made it even better. Tender and excellent. My kids nickname it "green fish."

Prep time: 20 minutes | Cook time: 10 minutes| Serves 4

- 1 pound mahi-mahi, cut into 1-inch pieces
- ¼ cup basil pesto
- 2 tablespoons extra-virgin olive oil
- 1 cup chopped cherry tomatoes
- ¼ cup pitted and quartered Taggiasca black olives
- Pinch sea salt
- 4 fresh basil leaves, chopped

1. In a large bowl, gently mix together the mahi-mahi and pesto, cover, and marinate in the refrigerator for at least 20 minutes.
2. In a large nonstick sauté pan or skillet over medium heat, warm the olive oil for 30 seconds. Add the marinated mahi-mahi, tomatoes, and salt. Cook, stirring occasionally, for 4 minutes. Add the olives and continue to cook, stirring occasionally, until the fish is cooked through, about 6 minutes. Remove from the heat and stir in the basil. Serve warm.
3. To make it more toddler-friendly: Cool to room temperature and skip the olives and fresh basil. Save them to garnish the top of the adult portions only.

Baked Salmon with Asparagus and Mushrooms

This recipe saves time on busy weeknights. In 10 minutes, you can cook a gourmet supper that everyone will eat. Salmon is healthful for kids, but its flavor may be too strong. Your kid will love it baked with honey-Dijon sauce.

Prep time: 10 minutes | Cook time: 20 minutes| Serves 4

- 1 (3-pound) salmon fillet
- 1 pound asparagus, trimmed
- 1 cup sliced cremini mushrooms
- 5 tablespoons extra-virgin olive oil
- 3 tablespoons Dijon mustard
- Juice of ½ lemon
- 1 tablespoon honey
- ½ teaspoon sea salt
- 4 garlic cloves, minced

1. Preheat the oven to 400°F. Line a baking sheet with parchment paper.
2. Pat the salmon dry with a paper towel and place it in the center of the prepared baking sheet. Place the asparagus and mushrooms on each side of the salmon.
3. To make it more toddler-friendly: Cut the asparagus into ½-inch pieces. It will be more tender and easier for kids to eat.
4. In a small bowl, whisk together the olive oil, mustard, lemon juice, honey, salt, and garlic. Pour the sauce over the salmon and drizzle it over the asparagus and mushrooms.
5. Bake for 15 minutes, then set the oven to broil and broil for 5 more minutes. Serve warm, or cooled to room temperature for toddlers.

Shrimp-Stuffed Zucchini Boats

Zucchini boats are always popular. After filling each with shrimp stuffing, add a basil leaf sail. After your child consumes the insides, they can eat the "boat."

Prep time: 15 minutes | Cook time: 35 minutes| Serves 4

- 6 zucchinis
- 3 tablespoons extra-virgin olive oil
- 1 garlic clove, minced
- Pinch sea salt
- ½ pound frozen cooked shrimp, thawed and chopped into small pieces
- ½ cup bread crumbs
- 2 fresh mint leaves, minced
- 1 teaspoon minced fresh parsley

1. Preheat the oven to 400°F. Line a baking sheet with parchment paper.
2. Cut 4 of the zucchinis in half lengthwise. Using a teaspoon, scoop out the inner pulp, place it in a bowl, and set it aside. Place the zucchini shells on the prepared baking sheet and bake for 15 minutes. Let cool on the baking sheet.
3. Chop the remaining 2 zucchinis into small pieces.
4. In a large sauté pan or skillet over medium heat, warm the olive oil, add the garlic, and cook for 1 minute. Add the chopped zucchini, the reserved zucchini pulp, and the salt and cook for 6 minutes. Remove from the heat, add the shrimp, breadcrumbs, mint, and parsley and mix to combine.
5. Fill the zucchini boats with the shrimp mixture and bake for another 15 minutes. Serve 2 boats to each person.

Sole and Bulgur–Stuffed Tomatoes

Stuffed tomatoes with bulgur and sole form a healthful supper. Kids may discover what's inside by lifting the tomato lid. Use two capers to make stuffed tomato eyes. Prepared bulgur can be refrigerated to save time.

Prep time: 15 minutes | Cook time: 40 minutes| Serves 4

- ½ cup bulgur
- 1 teaspoon sea salt, divided, plus more for seasoning
- ¾ cup water
- 4 heirloom tomatoes
- 4 sole fillets
- 1 garlic clove, minced
- 1 tablespoon minced fresh parsley
- 3 tablespoons extra-virgin olive oil

1. Preheat the oven to 400°F. Line a baking sheet with parchment paper.
2. In a medium saucepan over medium-high heat, mix together the bulgur, ½ teaspoon salt, and the water, and bring to a boil. Reduce the heat to medium-low and simmer, covered, until tender, about 12 minutes. Remove from the heat and let sit, covered, for 10 minutes. Fluff with a fork.
3. Cut off the top of each tomato to create a lid and set them aside. Using a spoon, scoop out the seeds and pulp.
4. Put the tomato pulp in a food processor and pulse several times to chop it. Squeeze out any extra liquid and put the tomato pulp in a bowl.
5. Place the sole fillets in the food processor and pulse a few times to chop them. Transfer the sole to the bowl with the tomatoes.
6. To make it more toddler-friendly: Pulse the sole fillets until they become a thick paste before transferring them to the bowl with the tomatoes.
7. Add the bulgur, garlic, parsley, and remaining ½ teaspoon salt to the bowl with the sole and tomatoes and stir to combine.
8. Place the hollowed-out tomatoes on the prepared baking sheet and sprinkle the insides with salt. Fill each tomato with the sole mix. Drizzle the olive oil over the top and cover with the tomato lids.
9. Bake for 25 to 30 minutes, until cooked through. Serve warm, or cooled to room temperature for toddlers.

Salmon and Zucchini Skewers

This recipe doesn't require grilling. These skewers can be stove-cooked. Zucchini marinated with salmon adds taste. Like colorful meals? Alternate zucchini, peppers, tomatoes, and onions.

Prep time: 10 minutes | Cook time: 10 minutes| Serves 4

- ½ cup extra-virgin olive oil
- ¼ cup lemon juice
- Zest of 1 lemon
- 8 garlic cloves, minced
- 2 tablespoons minced fresh dill
- 1 tablespoon honey
- 1½ teaspoons sea salt
- 1 pound skinless salmon, cut into 1-inch pieces
- 2 zucchinis, cut into 1-inch slices
- Have 6 skewers ready. For wood skewers, rinse them in water before using.

1. In a small bowl, mix together the olive oil, lemon juice, lemon zest, garlic, dill, honey, and salt. Add the salmon, mix together, and marinate for 5 minutes.
2. Place the salmon and zucchini onto the skewers, alternating between them.
3. Heat a large sauté pan or skillet over high heat for 1 minute. Add the skewers and cook for 3 to 4 minutes, flip, and continue to cook for another 3 minutes on the other side, until the salmon turns a pale pink.
4. For safety reasons, remove the salmon and zucchini from the skewers before serving them to kids. Serve 1 skewer for kids and 2 for adults.

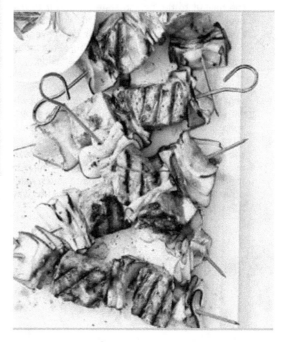

Fish Grain Bowl

This flavorful bowl is garnished with a fresh cilantro-yogurt sauce. Israeli couscous pearls are easier and less messy than ordinary couscous.

Prep time: 20 minutes | Cook time: 30 minutes| Serves 6

- 2 medium sweet potatoes, peeled and diced
- 1 medium head of broccoli, chopped with stems discarded
- 5 tablespoons extra-virgin olive oil, plus ½ cup, divided
- 3 garlic cloves, minced, divided
- 1 teaspoon sea salt, divided, plus more for seasoning
- ½ pound halibut, diced
- 1 cup packed fresh cilantro
- 1 tablespoon plain Greek yogurt
- 2 teaspoons honey
- Juice of ½ lemon
- 2 cups cooked Israeli couscous
- 1 cup shelled edamame
- 1 cup fresh baby spinach
- 2 scallions, chopped, for serving
- 1 tablespoon sesame seeds, for serving

1. Preheat the oven to 400°F. Line a baking sheet with parchment paper.
2. In a medium bowl, mix together the sweet potatoes, broccoli, 2 tablespoons olive oil, ⅓ of the minced garlic, and a pinch salt.
3. Transfer the mixture to the prepared baking sheet and roast for 20 minutes. Remove from the oven, but leave the oven on.
4. In a bowl, mix the halibut with 2 tablespoons olive oil, ⅓ of the minced garlic, and a pinch salt. Add the halibut to the baking sheet, return it to the oven, and bake for an additional 10 minutes.
5. In a food processor, process the cilantro, yogurt, ½ cup olive oil, honey, the remaining ½ teaspoon salt, and lemon juice until smooth. Set aside.
6. In a large bowl, gently mix together the Israeli couscous, edamame, baby spinach, roasted vegetables, and halibut. Serve in individual bowls with cilantro-yogurt dressing on top. For the adults, sprinkle the top with scallions and sesame seeds.
7. To make it more toddler-friendly: You can place the ingredients separately on a divided plate or even in a muffin tin, with the dressing on the side for kids who don't like their foods to touch each other. They can choose to mix and match any way they like.

Sheet Pan Tilapia with Potatoes, Tomatoes, and Olives

This flavorful one-pot (or baking sheet) supper is easy to make. Tilapia is a toddler-friendly fish, but the creamy almond crust makes it even better.

Prep time: 20 minutes | Cook time: 25 minutes| Serves 6

- 6 medium russet potatoes, thinly sliced
- 2 pounds tilapia fillets
- 5 tablespoons extra-virgin olive oil, divided
- ¼ cup bread crumbs
- ¼ cup grated Parmesan cheese
- ¼ cup almond meal
- 1 garlic clove, minced
- 1 tablespoon minced fresh parsley
- ½ teaspoon sea salt
- 1 cup cherry tomatoes
- 2 tablespoons pitted olives
- 4 ounces snow peas

1. Preheat the oven to 400°F. Line a baking sheet with parchment paper.
2. Place a layer of potatoes on the prepared baking sheet, placing them right next to each other. Place the tilapia fillets on top of the potatoes.
3. In a bowl, mix together 2 tablespoons olive oil, breadcrumbs, Parmesan cheese, almond meal, garlic, parsley, and salt. Sprinkle the tilapia with the breadcrumb mixture.
4. Place the cherry tomatoes and olives on top and the snow peas in between the fish fillets. Drizzle the remaining 3 tablespoons olive oil over the top.
5. Bake for 25 minutes, until cooked through.
6. To make it more toddler-friendly: Blend some of the potatoes, roasted cherry tomatoes, and olives together to make a "sauce" for the fish and snow peas. Add a few tablespoons of the cooking liquid from the baking sheet to thin the sauce and enhance the flavors.

Pork and Asparagus Tots with Tomato Salad

Fresh tomato and iceberg lettuce salad complements pork and asparagus tots. This recipe lets you make tots of any size. Make them little for kids and huge for parents. You can double the tots recipe and freeze them in an airtight container for up to 3 months.

Prep time: 15 minutes | Cook time: 15 minutes| Serves 6

- 1 pound fresh asparagus, trimmed
- 1 pound ground pork
- 2 sweet Italian sausages
- ¼ cup grated Parmesan cheese
- 3 fresh mint leaves, minced
- ¼ teaspoon sea salt, divided
- ½ cup unbleached all purpose flour
- 6 tablespoons extra-virgin olive oil, divided
- ½ medium head iceberg lettuce, shredded
- 3 heirloom tomatoes, chopped
- 4 fresh basil leaves, minced

1. In a food processor, pulse the asparagus for 30 seconds until it has the consistency of breadcrumbs. Transfer to a large bowl, add the ground pork, sausage, Parmesan cheese, mint, and ⅛ teaspoon salt and mix well to combine.
2. Pour the flour into a shallow bowl. With your hands, form the tots using 1 teaspoon of the pork mixture for each one, and dredge them in the flour.
3. In a large sauté pan or skillet over medium-high heat, warm 3 tablespoons olive oil. Add the tots and cook until browned on all sides, about 5 minutes. Reduce the heat to medium-low and continue cooking for an additional 5 minutes. If the liquid evaporates, you can add 3 tablespoons water to keep the tots from sticking.
4. In a bowl, mix together the lettuce, tomatoes, basil, the remaining 3 tablespoons olive oil, and the remaining ⅛ teaspoon salt.
5. Serve the tots with the salad on the side.

Stir-Fried Beef and Spinach

This is a great midweek dinner served over brown rice or quinoa. Add mushrooms, snow peas, broccoli, carrots, or shrimp for a surf-and-turf meal.

Prep time: 20 minutes | Cook time: 10 minutes| Serves 4

- 1 pound flank steak or sirloin, cut into thin slices
- ½ cup beef broth
- ⅓ cup soy sauce
- 3 tablespoons lemon juice
- 2 tablespoons tapioca starch
- 1 teaspoon grated fresh ginger
- 1 tablespoon honey
- 2 tablespoons extra-virgin olive oil
- 2 garlic cloves, minced
- 3 cups packed spinach, chopped

1. In a large bowl, mix together the steak, broth, soy sauce, lemon juice, tapioca starch, ginger, and honey, then cover and place in the refrigerator to marinate for 15 minutes.
2. In a large sauté pan or skillet over medium-high heat, warm the olive oil. Add the garlic and the marinated steak. Reserve the marinade and set aside. Cook, stirring occasionally, until browned, about 3 minutes. Transfer the steak to a bowl and set aside.
3. Add the spinach and the marinade to the skillet and cook, stirring, for 3 minutes. Add the steak back to the skillet, stir, and cook for 1 minute. Serve immediately.

Beef and Veggie–Stuffed Zucchini

It's fun if your food's bowl is edible. Kids enjoy this stuffing in zucchini shells. The container can be eaten after the filling. Baked zucchini can be frozen for 3 months in an airtight container.

Prep time: 15 minutes | Cook time: 35 minutes| Serves 4

- 4 zucchinis
- Pinch sea salt
- 1 red onion, chopped
- 1 garlic clove
- ½ pound ground beef
- 3 tablespoons extra-virgin olive oil, divided
- 1 eggplant, peeled, hollowed out, and diced
- 1 carrot, peeled and diced
- 3 tablespoons grated Parmesan cheese, plus more for topping
- 4 fresh basil leaves, chopped
- 1 tablespoon minced fresh parsley
- 1 to 2 tablespoons bread crumbs (optional)

1. Preheat the oven to 400°F.
2. Cut the zucchinis in half lengthwise. Then with a spoon, scoop out the insides and place in a food processor. Season the insides of the hollowed-out zucchinis with the salt, place in a baking pan, and set aside.
3. Add the onion and garlic to the food processor and pulse for 10 seconds.
4. Transfer the mixture to a large sauté pan or skillet. Add the ground beef and 2 tablespoons olive oil, and cook, stirring frequently, for 5 minutes. Add the eggplant and carrot to the skillet and continue to cook for 6 more minutes.
5. Remove from the heat. Add the Parmesan cheese, basil, and parsley and stir to combine.
6. If the final mixture is too watery (each zucchini has a different amount of liquid), add 1 or 2 tablespoons of breadcrumbs.
7. Spoon the filling into a hollowed-out zucchini half. Top each zucchini with 1 teaspoon of Parmesan cheese and a drizzle of olive oil and bake for 25 minutes, until cooked through and the cheese starts to brown.

Pancetta and Provolone Pork Rolls

Sage and rosemary enhance these creamy pork rolls. For adults, add 2 teaspoons balsamic vinegar towards the end. Add 1 cup thawed, drained frozen spinach to the fillings for added nutrition and moisture.

Prep time: 10 minutes | Cook time: 20 minutes| Serves 6

12 (⅛-inch-thick) pork loin slices
12 slices pancetta
12 slices provolone cheese
12 fresh sage leaves
¼ cup extra-virgin olive oil
2 garlic cloves, cut in half
½ cup chicken broth
2 fresh rosemary sprigs
Pinch sea salt
Have 12 to 15 water soaked toothpicks ready.

1. On a clean work surface, lay out the pork slices. Place 1 slice of pancetta, 1 slice of provolone, and 1 sage leaf on top of each slice of pork. Roll up the pork and secure with a toothpick.
2. In a large sauté pan or skillet over medium-high heat, warm the olive oil. Add the garlic and cook for 1 minute. Add the pork rolls and sear, turning to sear all sides, for 4 minutes. Add the broth, rosemary, and salt, then reduce the heat to medium-low and simmer for an additional 15 minutes. Remove the toothpicks and serve.
3. To make it more toddler-friendly: Cut the rolls into thin slices, which will be easier for little ones to chew.

Apple Rosemary Meatballs with Parmesan Cauliflower Mash

And beef? Lightly sweet apples are ideal for toddlers and adults alike. Pink Lady apples pair wonderfully with steak, but you may also use Fuji or Golden Delicious. Cauliflower mash is a creamy, light alternative to mashed potatoes. I prefer it with meatballs. Freezer-friendly meatballs. Before cooking, place in an airtight container and freeze for 3 months.

Prep time: 10 minutes | Cook time: 20 minutes| Serves 6

- 1 pound ground beef
- 1 Pink Lady apple, peeled, cored, and grated
- ½ cup bread crumbs
- ½ cup milk, divided
- 1 medium egg
- 1 garlic clove, minced
- 1 teaspoon minced fresh parsley
- Pinch sea salt
- 3 tablespoons extra-virgin olive oil
- 2 small rosemary sprigs
- 1½ cups water
- 1 medium head cauliflower cut into florets, chopped, and stems discarded
- ½ cup grated Parmesan cheese

1. Line a plate with paper towels.
2. In a large bowl, mix together the ground beef, apple, breadcrumbs, ¼ cup milk, egg, garlic, parsley, and salt and thoroughly combine.
3. Using your hands, form 1 tablespoon of the mixture into a ball. Repeat with the rest of the mixture.
4. In a large sauté pan or skillet over medium-high heat, warm the olive oil. Add the meatballs and sear, turning them to cook on all sides, for 3 minutes. Add the rosemary sprigs, reduce the heat to medium-low, and cook for an additional 5 minutes. Transfer the meatballs to the prepared plate. Discard the rosemary.
5. Place a steamer insert in a large pot, add the water, and bring to a boil over high heat. Add the cauliflower to the steamer, reduce the heat to medium, and steam the florets until tender, about 10 minutes.
6. Transfer the cauliflower to a bowl, add the Parmesan cheese and the remaining ¼ cup milk, and mash until the mixture looks like mashed potatoes.
7. Serve the meatballs with spoonfuls of cauliflower mash on the side.

Wintry Beef and Vegetable Stew

Cool weather calls for stew. If you cut the meat into little pieces, you can serve this in less than an hour. For a Mediterranean flavor, serve with couscous.

Prep time: 15 minutes | Cook time: 45 minutes| Serves 4

- 1 pound lean stew beef, diced
- ¼ cup unbleached all purpose flour
- 5 tablespoons extra-virgin olive oil, divided
- ½ white onion, minced
- 4 potatoes, peeled and diced
- 1½ cups beef broth
- Pinch sea salt
- 7 ounces frozen sweet peas
- 1 carrot, peeled and diced
- 1 tablespoon tomato paste

1. In a large bowl, toss the beef with the flour until evenly coated.
2. In a large sauté pan or skillet over medium heat, warm 3 tablespoons olive oil. Add the onion and cook for 2 minutes. Add the beef and sear, stirring frequently, for 3 minutes. Add the potatoes, beef broth, and salt, stir to combine, and cook for 3 minutes. Stir in the peas and diced carrots. Cover and simmer for 35 minutes.
3. Add the tomato paste and the remaining 2 tablespoons olive oil and mix well. Serve warm.
4. To make it more toddler-friendly: The ingredients are diced, so most toddlers will find this dish easy to eat, but you can also pulse the cooked stew a few times with an immersion blender, which will make the stew creamier. Serve at room temperature.

Skillet Steak with Tomato and Olives

The steak is flavored with olives, capers, oregano, and garlic. Cut a nice skirt steak into little pieces for your youngster. Mincing the olives and capers can make this dinner more toddler-friendly.

Prep time: 10 minutes | Cook time: 10 minutes | Serves 4

- 2 tablespoons chopped Taggiasca olives
- 1 tablespoon capers
- 1 celery stalk, roughly chopped
- 1 teaspoon dried oregano
- 3 tablespoons extra-virgin olive oil
- 1 garlic clove
- 4 skirt steak pieces (20 ounces total)
- 1 cup tomato sauce
- Pinch sea salt

1. In a food processor, pulse the olives, capers, celery, and oregano for 10 seconds.
2. In a large sauté pan or skillet over medium heat, warm the olive oil. Add the garlic and cook for 1 minute. Remove the garlic and discard.
3. Increase the heat to medium-high, add the steaks to the skillet, and cook for 3 minutes. Flip the steaks and add the tomato sauce, salt, and olive mixture on top. Reduce the heat to medium-low, cover, and cook for 5 to 6 minutes. Slice and serve immediately.

Bacon, Sweet Pea, and Mushroom Macaroni

Rich and salty bacon penetrates the mushrooms, making them more appealing to toddlers. Refrain from chopping mushrooms for your toddler. Thinly slice to preserve form. Your kids will learn to love mushrooms with time and exposure.

Prep time: 15 minutes | Cook time: 10 minutes | Serves 6

- 6 slices bacon (or pancetta or ham), diced
- ½ yellow onion, minced
- 3 garlic cloves, minced
- 1 pound frozen sweet peas
- 1 cup cremini mushrooms, thinly sliced
- 1 tablespoon minced fresh parsley
- Pinch sea salt
- 1 pound macaroni pasta
- 3 tablespoons grated Parmesan cheese, for serving

1. To make it more toddler-friendly: Pulse the bacon in a food processor for a few seconds. If the pieces are too big, they might be too chewy for little ones.
2. In a large sauté pan or skillet over medium heat, cook the bacon, onion, and garlic until the bacon is browned, about 5 minutes. Add the peas and mushrooms and stir to combine. Add the parsley and salt, stir, and cook for an additional 5 minutes.
3. Bring a large pot of water to a boil over high heat. Add the pasta and cook according to the package instructions. Drain the pasta, reserving 1 cup of the pasta water.
4. Add the pasta to the mixture in the skillet and stir to combine. If the sauce seems too thick, add the pasta water, 1 tablespoon at a time, until it reaches the desired consistency. Serve with a generous handful of Parmesan cheese on top.

Beef and Zucchini Pasta Bolognese

This is a vegetable Bolognese. It's an excellent method to blend meat and veggies for a healthier, tastier sauce. When I'm cooking, my kids keep sneaking teaspoons of this sauce to try. Use turkey or chicken instead of red meat. The sauce goes well with tagliatelle, although your kid may have trouble rolling it on a fork. Substitute fusilli, shells, or bowties.

Prep time: 10 minutes | Cook time: 30 minutes | Serves 6

- 1 yellow onion, minced
- 1 carrot, peeled and minced
- 1 celery stalk, minced
- 2 garlic cloves, minced
- 3 tablespoons extra-virgin olive oil
- 1 pound ground beef
- 1 pound zucchini, finely grated and drained
- 1 cup tomato sauce
- Pinch sea salt, plus 1 tablespoon, divided
- ½ cup warm water
- 1 pound tagliatelle pasta
- ¼ cup grated Parmesan cheese, for serving
- Pulse the onion, carrot, celery, and garlic in a food processor until minced.

1. In a large sauté pan or skillet over medium heat, warm the olive oil for 1 minute. Add the carrot mixture and cook for 3 minutes. Add the ground beef and cook, stirring frequently, for 5 minutes. Add the zucchini, tomato sauce, salt, and warm water, stir to combine, and bring to a boil. Reduce the heat to medium-low and simmer, uncovered, until the sauce reduces a bit, about 20 minutes.
2. To make it more toddler-friendly: If your toddler likes a super smooth texture, once the Bolognese sauce is cooked, use an immersion blender to transform it into a smooth purée.
3. Fill a large pot with water and bring to a boil over high heat. Add the pasta and the remaining 1 tablespoon salt. Cook according to the package instructions. Drain the pasta, reserving 1 cup of pasta water.
4. Combine the pasta with the Bolognese. If the sauce is too thick, add the reserved pasta water, 1 tablespoon at a time, until it reaches the desired consistency. Serve warm, or cooled to room temperature for toddlers, with a generous handful of Parmesan cheese on top.

Southwestern Quinoa Salad

Colorful quinoa. Any hue can be used, but I prefer mixed. Red and black quinoa are heartier than white. This salad is perfect for family meals or potlucks. Always popular.

Prep time: 5 minutes | Cook time: 5 minutes | Serves 6

- 3 cups cooked quinoa
- 1 large bell pepper, diced
- 11 ounces fresh or frozen corn niblets
- 1 (15-ounce) can black beans, drained and rinsed
- 4 green onions, sliced
- ⅓ cup olive oil
- 2 teaspoons lime zest
- ½ cup lime juice
- 1 teaspoon kosher salt
- Black pepper

1. In a large mixing bowl, stir together the quinoa, bell pepper, corn, black beans, green onions, olive oil, lime zest, lime juice, salt, and pepper. Serve.

Cheesy Beef and Spinach Baked Pasta

Baked spinach meatballs and pasta are delicious and warm. The taste combination is toddler-friendly, while the iron- and omega-3-rich meatballs make mom pleased.

Prep time: 20 minutes | Cook time: 30 minutes| Serves 6

- ½ pound ground beef
- ¼ cup ricotta cheese
- 3 tablespoons grated Parmesan cheese, plus ½ cup, divided
- 1 cup frozen spinach, thawed and finely chopped
- 1 teaspoon garlic powder
- ¼ teaspoon ground nutmeg
- 1 tablespoon chia seeds
- Pinch sea salt
- 3 tablespoons extra-virgin olive oil
- ¾ cup tomato sauce

1. Preheat the oven to 400°F. Have a 9-by-13-inch baking dish ready.
2. Fill a large pot with water and bring to a boil. Cook the pasta for 5 minutes less than the package instructions suggest. Drain, reserving 1 cup of pasta water.
3. In a large bowl, mix together the ground beef, ricotta, 3 tablespoons Parmesan cheese, spinach, garlic, nutmeg, chia seeds, and salt.
4. Using your hands, form 1 tablespoon of the mixture into a ball. Repeat with the rest of the mixture. Place the meatballs in the baking dish. Drizzle the olive oil on top and bake for 20 minutes.
5. Add the pasta and tomato sauce to the baking dish and stir to combine. If the sauce is too thick, add the pasta water, 1 tablespoon at a time, until it reaches the desired consistency. Top with the remaining ½ cup Parmesan cheese.
6. Place the baking dish back in the oven for an additional 10 minutes. Adjust the oven to broil and bake for 3 minutes, until the cheese is golden. Serve hot.

Broccoli and Sausage Risotto

Risotto is ideal for babies since the rice releases its starch when cooked in a flavorful broth. This is my kids' and my favorite risotto because it's healthy and balanced.

Prep time: 15 minutes | Cook time: 25 minutes| Serves 4

- 5 to 6 cups chicken broth
- 3 tablespoons extra-virgin olive oil
- ½ sweet white onion, minced
- 3 sweet Italian sausages
- 1 head broccoli, cut into florets, chopped, and stems discarded
- 1½ cups Arborio or carnaroli rice
- ¼ cup grated Parmesan cheese
- 2 tablespoons plain Greek yogurt

1. In a large pot over low heat, warm the broth.
2. In another large pot over medium-high heat, warm the olive oil. Add the onion and cook for 2 minutes. Add the sausage, breaking it up with a spoon, and cook for 2 minutes. Add the broccoli and cook for an additional 2 minutes. Add the rice, stir for 1 minute, and add 3 ladles of broth. Set a timer at 18 minutes.
3. Cook, stirring constantly, until the liquid is almost absorbed. Continue to add the broth, one ladle at a time, letting the liquid absorb after each addition.
4. When the timer goes off, the rice should be cooked. Remove from the heat, add the Parmesan cheese and Greek yogurt, and stir to combine. Serve warm, or cooled to room temperature for toddlers.

Ham and Kale Dumplings

This is a toddler-friendly variation of "naked dumplings," or gnudi. These dumplings aren't packed with pasta. Eggs bond greens, cheese, and ham, and bread keeps them wet and fluffy.

Prep time: 15 minutes | Cook time: 7 minutes| Serves 4

- 1 tablespoon sea salt, plus extra for sprinkling
- 1 tablespoon extra-virgin olive oil, plus extra for drizzling
- 10 ounces kale, stems removed and chopped
- 7 ounces day-old bread
- 1 thick slice of ham, diced
- 2 medium eggs
- ⅔ cup whole milk
- ⅔ cup grated Parmesan cheese, plus 2 tablespoons, divided
- 3 ounces Manchego cheese, diced
- 3 tablespoons bread crumbs

1. Fill a large pot with water. Bring to a boil over high heat and add 1 tablespoon salt. Reduce the heat to keep the water just boiling.
2. In a large sauté pan or skillet over medium-high heat, warm 1 tablespoon olive oil for 1 minute. Add the kale, sprinkle with salt, and cook for 2 to 3 minutes until the volume of the kale reduces to less than half. Let cool for 5 minutes.
3. Transfer the kale to a food processor, add the bread, and process for 1 minute.
4. In a large bowl, mix together the kale mixture, ham, eggs, milk, Parmesan cheese, Manchego cheese, and breadcrumbs.
5. To make it more toddler-friendly: For kids who don't like a lot of texture, add the diced ham to the food processor with the kale and bread, and blend until smooth before mixing with the eggs, milk, cheeses, and breadcrumbs.
6. Using your hands, form small balls and place them on a plate. Add them to the boiling water and cook for 3 minutes. They will rise to the surface of the water when they are cooked. Using a slotted spoon, transfer the dumplings to a serving bowl.
7. Serve with a drizzle of olive oil and a sprinkle of Parmesan cheese.

Peach Toast with Maple Tahini

Toddlers love bread with toppings. You can use other in-season soft fruits instead of peaches. This snack has protein, lipids, and fiber from tahini, peach, and bread.

Prep time: 10 minutes|Cook time:5 minutes | Serves 1

- 1 whole-grain bread slice, toasted and halved
- ½ peach, thinly sliced
- 2 tablespoons tahini
- 1 tablespoon pure maple syrup

1. Arrange the toast on a plate. Put the peach slices on top of the toast.
2. In a small bowl, whisk together the tahini and syrup. Drizzle over the peaches.

Chapter 7
Super Foods Recipes

Introducing solid foods to your baby could be challenging, and could become more difficult when you have to introduce superfoods. You must understand your baby's hunger levels and determine whether you prefer using homemade foods or processed foods. The more the baby grows, the more it needs snacks, more regular meals and an even greater variety of foods. We are here to hold your hand through this journey. Seeing your baby happy gives us joy. Our super easy recipes will help walk you through most of these bonus foods. For example, baked superfoods. You can always whip up something using healthy ingredients such as black beans, spinach and even quinoa. It is not always that baked means sugars or spices. Nutritious smoothies could be another way to serve a bonus superfood, and the good news is that these ingredients are readily available. For example, avocado, blueberries and spinach. Add a liquid of your choice, which could be breast milk or probiotic Greek-style yogurt. Ready to serve!

Maple Spice Pepita Trail Mix

Pepitas are hulled pumpkin seeds high in fiber, protein, potassium, iron, and magnesium. When cooked with maple syrup and cranberries, they're excellent. This combination will last a week at room temperature if sealed.

Prep time: 5 minutes|Cook time:20 minutes| Serves 4

- 1 cup pepitas
- 3 tablespoons pure maple syrup
- ¼ teaspoon ground ginger
- ¼ cup dried cranberries
- Pinch sea salt

1. Preheat the oven to 300°F. Line a rimmed baking sheet with parchment paper.
2. In a small bowl, mix the pepitas, maple syrup, and ginger. Spread in a single layer on the prepared baking sheet.
3. Bake for about 20 minutes, stirring once or twice, until golden.
4. Return to the bowl. Stir in the cranberries and season with the salt.

Sweet Potato Toasts with Avocado

Sweet potato toasts are a simple snack you can customize with toppings. Toasts can be made in advance. Reheat them in the toaster after storing them in the fridge for a week.

Prep time: 5 minutes|Cook time:10 minutes | Serves 4

- ½ sweet potato, peeled and sliced lengthwise into ¼-inch-thick slices
- ¼ avocado, mashed
- 2 teaspoons freshly squeezed lime juice
- Pinch sea salt

1. In a toaster, heat the slices of sweet potatoes for 5 to 10 minutes, until cooked through and tender. You may need to pop them back in the toaster a few times depending on your toaster settings.
2. In a small bowl, mash the avocado with the lime and salt.
3. Spread on the sweet potato toasts just before serving.3

Roasted Delicata Squash with Honey Butter

These squash slices are excellent warm or cold. Your youngster will adore the light, sweet flavor of these 5-day snacks.

Prep time: 5 minutes|Cook time:20 minutes | Serves 4

- 1 delicata squash, halved lengthwise and cut into ¼-to ½-inch-thick slices
- 1 tablespoon unsalted butter, melted
- 1 tablespoon honey
- ¼ teaspoon ground cinnamon
- Pinch sea salt

1. Preheat the oven to 350°F. Line a rimmed baking sheet with parchment paper.
2. In a large bowl, toss the squash with the butter, honey, cinnamon, and salt. Spread in a single layer on the prepared baking sheet.
3. Bake for 20 minutes, turning once, until tender.

Beet Applesauce

Applesauce is how I found this recipe. Apples complement beets' sweet, earthy flavor. A excellent on-the-go snack. Until 6 months, freeze or refrigerate.

Prep time: 5 minutes|Cook time:30 minutes | Serves 4

- 2 beets, peeled and chopped
- 3 sweet-tart apples, such as Braeburn, peeled, cored, and chopped
- 1 tablespoon freshly squeezed lemon juice
- ½ teaspoon ground cinnamon
- ½ teaspoon fresh ginger, grated
- Pinch sea salt

1. In a large pot, combine the beets and ½ cup water. Simmer for 15 minutes, uncovered, stirring occasionally.
2. Add the apples, lemon juice, cinnamon, ginger, and salt. Simmer for 10 to 15 minutes, stirring occasionally, until saucy.
3. Cool slightly and, if desired, blend with an immersion blender, in a food processor, or in a blender to make the sauce smooth.

Carrot Fries with Citrus-Tahini Dipping Sauce

Potato-based fries? Who says? Carrots give these baked fries a French fry-like texture. Homemade Ketchup replaces tahini.

Prep time: 10 minutes|Cook time:20 minutes | Serves 4

- 3 carrots, peeled, halved crosswise, and cut into ½-inch spears
- 2 tablespoons extra-virgin olive oil
- ¼ teaspoon sea salt
- ¼ cup tahini
- 1 garlic clove, minced
- 3 tablespoons freshly squeezed lemon or orange juice
- 2 tablespoons fresh parsley, chopped
- Salt

1. Preheat the oven to 425°F.
2. In a bowl, toss the carrots with the olive oil. Spread in a single layer on a rimmed baking sheet.
3. Bake for 10 minutes. Flip and continue cooking until crispy, about 10 minutes more.
4. Season with the salt.
5. In a small bowl, whisk together the tahini, garlic, lemon juice, parsley, and 2 tablespoons water. Taste and season with salt. Serve the fries with the dipping sauce on the side.

Chewy Nut-Free Granola Bars

These gluten-free bars are allergen-free. They're easy to make and keep for a week at room temperature. Lunchboxes, toddlers, and older siblings love them.

Prep time: 10 minutes|Cook time:15 minutes | Serves 8

- 2 cups rolled oats
- ⅔ cup ground flaxseed
- 1 cup dried dates, chopped
- 1 cup dried apples, chopped
- ½ cup extra-virgin olive oil
- ½ cup pure maple syrup
- ¼ cup raw honey

1. Preheat the oven to 350°F. Line a 9-by-13-inch baking pan with parchment paper.
2. In a large bowl, mix together the oats, flaxseed, dates, apples, olive oil, maple syrup, and honey. Press into the prepared baking pan.
3. Bake for 15 minutes, until golden.
4. Cut into squares to serve.

Pumpkin Energy Balls

These no-bake pumpkin balls freeze wonderfully, making them excellent on-the-go snacks for your child (and the whole family). You may add anything to energy bites. Try adding shredded coconut, dried fruit, or cacao powder. Gluten-free oats keep them allergen-free.

Prep time: 10 minutes | Serves 10

- 1½ cups gluten-free rolled oats
- ½ cup sun butter
- ½ cup pumpkin purée
- ¼ cup ground flaxseed
- ¼ cup honey
- ½ teaspoon pumpkin pie spice
- Pinch sea salt

1. Line a baking sheet with parchment paper.
2. In a medium bowl, combine the oats, sun butter, pumpkin purée, flaxseed, honey, pumpkin pie spice, and salt, mixing well.
3. Form the mixture into 1-tablespoon balls and place on the prepared tray. Serve immediately, or transfer to an airtight container and store, refrigerated, for up to 1 week.

Avocado Fries

Children love the delicate texture and crispy coating of these baked avocado snacks. Serve with ranch dressing or another favorite for a fun toddler snack.

Prep time: 10 minutes|Cook time:15 minutes | Serves 4

- 1 avocado, cut into lengthwise spears
- Juice of ¼ lime
- ¼ cup almond flour
- ½ teaspoon sea salt
- 1 egg, beaten

1. Preheat the oven to 400°F. Line a baking sheet with parchment paper.
2. Sprinkle lime juice over the avocado pieces.
3. In a small bowl, combine the almond flour and sea salt.
4. In a small bowl, whisk the egg.
5. Dip the avocado pieces into the egg and then into the almond flour mixture.
6. Arrange on the prepared baking sheet. Bake for 15 minutes, or until crisp.

Pumpkin Muffin Minis

You can multitask while these little muffins bake. They last 1 week firmly sealed and 6 months frozen. So make these on the weekend for a quick, nutritious snack for your kid. Julian adores these frozen treats.

Prep time: 10 minutes|Cook time:15 minutes | Serves 12

coconut oil, melted, for greasing
2 cups gluten-free rolled oats
2 tablespoons hemp hearts
½ teaspoon ground cinnamon
¼ teaspoon ground nutmeg
Pinch sea salt
Pinch baking powder
1 cup pumpkin purée
1 large egg, beaten
nondairy milk¼ cup pure maple syrup
½ teaspoon vanilla extract

1. Preheat the oven to 350°F. Brush the muffin tins lightly with melted coconut oil.
2. In a large bowl, whisk together the oats, hemp hearts, cinnamon, nutmeg, salt, and baking powder.
3. In another bowl, whisk together the pumpkin, egg, milk, maple syrup, and vanilla.
4. Add the wet ingredients to the dry, mixing until just combined.
5. Spoon into the prepared muffin tins. Bake for 12 to 15 minutes, until a toothpick inserted in the center comes out clean.

Yogurt-Dipped Frozen Bananas

Toddlers love decorating frozen bananas. Your child can decorate them with coconut, raisins, or micro chocolate chips. Julian adored my Halloween ghosts with raisins for eyes. These snacks use ice pop sticks or wooden skewers. Before building, cut the sharp end off wooden skewers.

Prep time: 10 minutes, plus 3 to 6 hours freezing time |
Serves 4

- 2 bananas, halved lengthwise
- 1 cup plain whole-milk yogurt
- 2 tablespoons pure maple syrup
- ½ teaspoon ground cinnamon

1. Line a baking sheet with parchment paper.
2. Insert ice pop sticks or skewers into the bananas along the cut edge.
3. In a medium bowl, whisk together the yogurt, maple syrup, and cinnamon.
4. Dip the bananas in the yogurt, coating them. Arrange on the prepared baking sheet.
5. Decorate as desired.
6. Freeze for 3 to 6 hours or until the yogurt is set.

Banana Sushi Bites

Baby sushi? Banana and tortillas? Sure. These interesting shapes are a terrific way to provide food to your toddler in a new way. Serve with a honey-yogurt sauce for dipping.

Prep time: 10 minutes | Serves 2

2 tablespoons cashew or almond butter
1 whole-wheat tortilla
1 banana, peeled
Pinch ground cinnamon, for garnish

1. Spread the cashew butter on the tortilla.
2. Place the banana on the nut butter and roll, using a bit more nut butter to glue the edges shut.
3. Cut into 1½-inch-thick slices. Garnish with cinnamon.

Zucchini Dip with Veggies

Zucchini makes an excellent dip foundation without heating or roasting. Mix it in a blender or food processor with spices and tahini for a great-tasting veggie-based dip your child can use to dip other raw nutrient-packed vegetables.

Prep time: 10 minutes | Serves 4

- 1 medium zucchini, roughly chopped
- 1 tablespoon freshly squeezed lemon juice
- 1 garlic clove, minced
- 2 tablespoons tahini
- 2 tablespoons extra-virgin olive oil
- 1 tablespoon fresh parsley, chopped
- Pinch sea salt
- Pinch paprika
- 1 cucumber, peeled and cut into sticks

1. In a blender or food processor jar, combine the zucchini, lemon juice, garlic, tahini, olive oil, parsley, salt, and paprika. Process until smooth.
2. Serve with the cucumber sticks for dipping.

Avocado Dipping Sauce

This three-ingredient sauce will become a favorite once you learn how easy it is to make. Use this to dip Cauliflower Tots, Celery Root and Sweet Potato Cakes, or cut vegetables for a tasty snack.

Prep time: 10 minutes | Makes about ¼ cup

- ½ avocado
- 1 teaspoon freshly squeezed lime juice
- ½ teaspoon minced garlic

1. In a small bowl, combine the avocado, lime juice, and garlic. Using a fork, mash the avocado, mixing it together with the lime juice and garlic.
2. Add a little water, 1 teaspoon at a time, if necessary, to adjust the consistency. Serve with vegetables for dipping. Store remaining dipping sauce in the refrigerator.

Maple Butternut Butter

This apple butter is different. Roasting gives squash a rich, sweet earthiness that complements maple. Serve it on whole-grain bread or as a dip for fruit pieces. This can be refrigerated for 5 days or frozen for 6 months.

Prep time: 5 minutes|Cook time:25 minutes| Serves 6

- 1 butternut squash, rind removed and cut into ½-inch cubes
- 1 tablespoon extra-virgin olive oil
- ¼ cup pure maple syrup
- ½ teaspoon ground cinnamon
- 2 tablespoons freshly squeezed orange juice
- Pinch salt

1. Preheat the oven to 425°F.
2. In a mixing bowl, toss the squash with the olive oil. Spread in a single layer on a rimmed baking sheet.
3. Bake for 20 to 25 minutes, until soft.
4. Transfer the squash to the blender or food processor along with the maple syrup, cinnamon, orange juice, and salt. Blend until smooth.

Veggie Purée Pouches

Remember making baby purées? In reusable pouches, they make great on-the-go munchies. You can combine fruits and vegetables and add herbs and spices. You can heat the purées, thin them, and serve them as soup or soup foundation with cut-up veggies. Even 4- and 5-year-olds love pouches.

Prep time: 5 minutes|Cook time:10 minutes| Serves 4

- 1 cup diced vegetables (such as carrots, peas, or turnips)
- ½ cup diced, peeled fruit (such as apples or pears)
- ¼ cup liquid (such as unsalted vegetable broth, water, or milk)
- ½ teaspoon dried herbs or spices
- Pinch salt

1. Fill a large saucepan with 1 inch of water and insert a steamer basket. Bring the water to a boil.
2. Add the vegetables and fruit to the steamer basket and steam for 10 minutes, until soft.
3. Transfer to a blender or food processor. Add the liquid, a couple tablespoons at a time, along with the herbs and salt. Purée until smooth, adjusting the thickness by adding more liquid as needed.

Cucumber Mango Mint Ice Pops

I adore ice pops for children since they're refreshing, easy to eat, and can contain many healthful ingredients. They're great when your child's teeth are bugging her.

Prep time: 10 minutes, plus about 6 hours freezing time| Serves 4

- 1 cucumber, peeled and chopped
- 1 mango, peeled and cubed
- 1 tablespoon fresh mint, chopped
- 1 cup apple juice or white grape juice

1. In a blender or food processor, combine the cucumber, mango, mint, and juice. Blend until smooth.
2. Pour into a four-serving ice pop mold and freeze for about 6 hours, or until frozen.

Dairy-Free Fudgesicles

These creamy delights replace ice cream. Your child will love them, and he can assist measure and stir ingredients. Maple syrup sweetens these fudgesicles.

Prep time: 5 minutes, plus about 6 hours freezing time| Serves 4

- 1 cup canned coconut milk
- ½ cup unsweetened cacao powder
- 6 tablespoons pure maple syrup

1. In a liquid measuring cup, whisk together the coconut milk, cacao powder, and maple syrup until well combined.
2. Pour into a four-serving ice pop mold and freeze for about 6 hours, or until frozen.

Avocado Chocolate Mousse

Who knew avocado worked in pudding-like recipes? Its creamy consistency makes it the perfect base for a dairy-free, cooked chocolate mousse.

Prep time: 5 minutes| Serves 2

- 1 avocado
- 2 tablespoons pure maple syrup
- ¼ cup unsweetened cacao powder
- ½ teaspoon vanilla extract
- Pinch salt

1. In a blender or food processor, combine the avocado, maple syrup, cacao powder, milk, vanilla, and salt. Blend until smooth and serve.

Banana Ice Cream with Chocolate Sauce

This banana ice cream contains only bananas. Creamy ice cream covered with chocolate sauce is the perfect toddler snack.

Prep time: 5 minutes| Serves 4

- 2 bananas, sliced and frozen
- ¼ cup melted coconut oil
- 2 tablespoons pure maple syrup
- 2 tablespoons unsweetened cacao powder
- Pinch sea salt

1. In a blender or food processor, blend the bananas until smooth.
2. In a small bowl, whisk together the coconut oil, maple syrup, cacao powder, and salt.
3. Spoon the chocolate sauce over the banana ice cream and serve.

Easy Peanut Butter Cookies

Gluten-free, four-ingredient cookies. If you don't have coconut sugar, you can use brown or white sugar. The texture needs granulated sugar, not honey or maple syrup.

Prep time: 5 minutes|Cook time:15 minutes| Makes 24 cookies

- 1 cup peanut butter
- ¼ cup coconut sugar
- 1 egg, beaten
- 1 teaspoon baking soda

1. Preheat the oven to 350°F. Line a baking sheet with parchment paper.
2. In a small bowl or mixer, mix the peanut butter, coconut sugar, egg, and baking soda.
3. Drop in 1-teaspoon balls onto the prepared baking sheet. Flatten slightly with a fork, making a cross-hatch pattern with the tines.
4. Bake for about 10 minutes, until browned.

Banana-Pineapple Ice Cream Sundaes

This easy banana-pineapple sauce can be refrigerated for up to 5 days and spooned over ice cream. Julian enjoys helping me prepare this fruity sauce, and the banana is great for practicing butter knife skills.

Prep time: 5 minutes|Cook time:5 minutes| Serves 4

- 2 tablespoons unsalted butter
- 1 banana, sliced
- 1 cup fresh or canned and drained pineapple, finely chopped
- ¼ cup pure maple syrup
- ½ teaspoon ground ginger
- Pinch salt
- 1 pint vanilla ice cream

1. In a large, nonstick skillet, melt the butter on medium high until it bubbles.
2. Add the banana and pineapple and cook for about 5 minutes, stirring occasionally, until the fruit begins to brown.
3. 3.Add the maple syrup, ginger, and salt. Simmer for 3 minutes. Serve spooned over the ice cream.

Apple Spice Celebration Cake with Maple Cream Cheese Icing

When celebrating, only cake will do. This sweet and tasty cake has less processed sugar than others.

Prep time: 30 minutes|Cook time:25 minutes|Serves 10

- For the cake
- ¾ cup coconut oil, melted
- ½ cup pure maple syrup
- ¼ cup unsweetened applesauce
- 2 large eggs, beaten
- 1 teaspoon vanilla extract
- 1½ cups cake flour
- ¼ cup coconut sugar
- ½ teaspoon baking powder
- ½ teaspoon baking soda
- Pinch sea salt
- 1 teaspoon ground ginger
- 1 teaspoon ground cinnamon
- ½ teaspoon ground cloves
- 2 apples, peeled, cored, and finely chopped
- For the frosting
- 6 ounces cream cheese, softened
- 3 tablespoons unsalted butter, softened
- ¼ cup pure maple syrup
- ¼ teaspoon vanilla extract
- To make the cake

1. Preheat the oven to 325°F. Grease and flour two (8-inch) round layer cake pans.
2. In a large bowl, beat together the coconut oil, maple syrup, applesauce, eggs, and vanilla.
3. In a medium bowl, sift together the cake flour, coconut sugar, baking powder, baking soda, salt, ginger, cinnamon, and cloves.
4. Add the dry ingredients to the wet and mix until just combined. Fold in the apples.
5. Spread evenly in the two prepared cake pans. Bake for about 20 minutes, until a toothpick inserted in the cake comes out clean. Cool on a wire rack.
6. When the cakes have cooled, turn out from the pans and rest on the wire rack until cool before frosting.

MAKE THE FROSTING

7. In a medium bowl, combine the cream cheese, butter, maple syrup, and vanilla. Beat until smooth.
8. To assemble the cake
9. Set one of the cake rounds on a cake plate and trim the top with a serrated knife to make it even. Using an offset spatula, ice around the sides and the top of the round.
10. Place the other cake round on top. Ice the sides and top.

Yogurt Bark

Yogurt bark is delicious. This simple, colorful recipe makes a fantastic snack, dessert, or breakfast. High in protein, low in sugar, perfect for kids and adults. Whole-milk yogurt is creamier.

Prep time: 5 minutes, plus 4 hours freezing time| Serves 4

- 2 cups plain whole-milk yogurt
- 2 tablespoons honey
- 1 teaspoon vanilla extract
- 2 tablespoons chocolate chips
- 2 tablespoons chopped strawberries
- 2 tablespoons pumpkin seeds (optional)

1. In a small bowl, mix the yogurt, honey, and vanilla. Pour onto a parchment paper-lined baking sheet.
2. Sprinkle the chocolate chips, strawberries, and/ or pumpkin seeds (if using) on top.
3. Freeze for at least 4 hours. Once frozen, break into pieces and transfer to an airtight container and store in the freezer.

Strawberries with Mexican Chocolate Yogurt Dip

Cinnamon and allspice flavor Mexican hot chocolate. We eliminate the cayenne that is sometimes added for heat. This mildly spicy, sweet dip tastes like Mexican hot chocolate and is great for dipping strawberries or other fruits.

Prep time: 5 minutes| Serves 2

- ½ cup plain whole-milk yogurt
- 2 tablespoons unsweetened cacao powder
- 1 tablespoon pure maple syrup
- ¼ teaspoon ground cinnamon
- Pinch allspice
- 1 cup sliced strawberries

1. In a small bowl, whisk together the yogurt, cacao powder, maple syrup, cinnamon, and allspice.
2. Serve with the strawberries (or another sliced fruit) for dipping.

Brownies

These dense brownies are fudgy. The recipe calls for coconut sugar, but you can substitute sugar (in equal amounts).

Prep time: 15 minutes|Cook time:25 minutes| Makes 9 brownies

- ¼ cup plus 1 tablespoon coconut oil, plus extra for greasing
- ¾ cup semisweet chocolate chips or chopped chocolate
- ¾ cup coconut sugar
- 2 large eggs, beaten
- 1½ teaspoons vanilla extract
- 2 tablespoons unsweetened cacao powder
- ½ teaspoon baking powder
- ¾ cup almond flour
- Pinch sea salt

1. Preheat the oven to 350°F. Grease an 8-inch square baking pan with coconut oil.
2. In a small saucepan, heat the chocolate chips, coconut oil, and coconut sugar on medium high, stirring constantly, until melted.
3. Remove from the heat and whisk in the eggs and vanilla.
4. In a small bowl, whisk together the cacao powder, baking powder, almond flour, and salt. Stir into the chocolate mixture until combined.
5. Spread in an even layer in the prepared baking pan. Bake for about 20 minutes, until a toothpick inserted in the center comes out clean. Cool before cutting into squares.

Kale Chips

Getting your child engaged in cooking gives them a stake in what you're producing, making them more likely to try it. My youngster loves helping me prepare kale chips. He shreds kale and adds seasonings.

Prep time: 5 minutes|Cook time:15 minutes| Serves 4

- 1 kale bunch, stemmed and torn into smaller pieces
- 1 tablespoon extra-virgin olive oil
- ½ teaspoon sea salt

1. Preheat the oven to 350°F. Line two rimmed baking sheets with parchment paper.
2. In a mixing bowl, toss the kale with the olive oil, and spread it in a single layer on the prepared baking sheets.
3. Bake for 10 to 15 minutes, until the edges brown.
4. Sprinkle with the salt while warm.

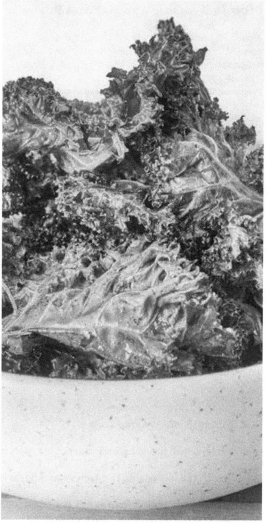

Basic Apple and Walnut Baby Purée

Apple Purée is a smooth, delicious first food for babies. It has protein, Omega 3, and walnuts.

Prep time: 1 minute | Cook time: 10 minutes | Serves 6

- 2 apples
- 1/4 cup walnuts, shelled
- 1/8 tsp ground cinnamon

1. Peel the apples and remove the core. Cut into chunks.
2. Steam the apple chunks and walnuts for 7 minutes or until the apples are tender. Keep steamer water and put aside.
3. In a food processor or blender, put the steamed apples, walnuts, cinnamon, and 3 tablespoons of the water from the steamer pot.
4. Purée for 3 minutes or until smooth.
5. Cool 10 minutes before serving.

Simple Avocado and Banana Purée

Want nutrient-rich infant food? Avocados and bananas are full of beta-carotene, vitamins C and E, magnesium, and potassium, and they taste delicious.

Prep time: 10 minutes | Cook time: no need to cook | Serves 8

- 2 avocados, ripe
- 2 bananas, ripe
- 2 tsp pineapple juice

1. Halve the avocado, remove pit, and use a spoon to scoop out the flesh.
2. Peel bananas and chop.
3. Put all ingredients in a food processor. Purée until smooth
4. For a texture-free Purée, use a food strainer to remove all the lumps.
5. Freeze in a freezer-safe container for up to 4 days.

Banana Mango Smoothie

Mango Purée boosts kids' immunity. Mango has Vitamin C and other minerals.

Prep time: 5 minutes | Cook time: no-cook needed | Serves 8

- 1 mango
- 1 banana
- 3 tbsp breast milk or formula milk

1. Peel the mango and banana, and cut the flesh in quarters.
2. Add all the ingredients to a blender and purée it until smooth.
3. Add the breastmilk or formula milk one tablespoon at a time until desired consistency is reached.

Stone-Fruit Purée

Plum and Apricot hybrid. This fruit's amusing name belies its great benefits. If you can't get pluots, replace 1 apricot and 1 plum.

Prep time: 1 minute | Cook time: no-cook needed | Serves 8

- 2 white peaches
- 2 pluots (or 1 apricot and 1 plum)

1. Make an X using a knife at the bottom of the peaches and pluots and cut through the flesh. Leave them whole.
2. Place the fruit in a steamer over boing water for 5 – 6 minutes or until the skin starts to peel off and the fruit is softened.
3. Take out the fruits to cool. Peel off the skin of the fruits.
4. Chop the fruit into chunks and disregard the pit. Put all the ingredients in a blender and Purée until smooth.

Sweet Potato Pudding

A creamy, light dessert or snack for babies. This recipe is so excellent that your whole family will adore it.

Prep time: 5 minutes | Cook time: 1 hour 30 minutes | Serves 3

- 1 sweet potato, medium
- 1 egg yolk
- 1/4 tsp cinnamon
- 1/4 cup almond milk
- Hot water

1. Preheat oven for 400°F.
2. Bake the sweet potato for 1 hour.
3. Remove the sweet potato and let cool. Remove the skin.
4. Whisk the egg with cinnamon, milk and sweet potato until smooth.
5. Place the mixture in a small baking bowl and put it into a larger baking pan.
6. Do the water bath method. Place the baking dish (with the bowl in it) inside the oven. Fill it halfway with hot water, so that interior bowl "floats".
7. Bake for another 30 minutes.
8. Cool at least 10 minutes before serving.

Banana Avocado Date Purée

Banana and avocado are fantastic first foods. They're sweet and thick when Puréed, and full of vitamins and minerals.

Prep time: 1 minute | Cook time: no-cook needed | Serves 3

- 1 banana, sliced
- 1/2 avocado, cubed
- 1 pitted date
- 2 tbsp breast milk, or formula milk

1. In a food processor, add all the ingredients and purée until thick, but smooth.

Tropical Fruit Purée

A revitalizing fruit Purée that is also good for your baby as a snack!

Prep time: 10 minutes | Cook time: no-cook needed | Serves 4 – 6

- 1-1/2 cups mango, ripe
- 1-1/2 cups papaya, ripe
- 1 large banana, chopped

1. Wash all fruit before removing skin.
2. Peel the mango and cut into chunks. Cut the papaya in half, remove the seeds and scoop out the flesh.
3. Place the fruits in a blender and blend until smooth.
4. Serve.

Pear and Apple Purée

Pear and apple include vitamin C and fiber to help your baby thrive. A great combination.

Prep time: 10 minutes | Cook time: 3 minutes | Serves 6

- 1 apple, peeled and cubed
- 1 pear, ripe, peeled and cubed
- 1/8 tsp cinnamon, ground

1. Steam the apple and pear cubes for 3 minutes until tender.
2. Place all the ingredients in a blender or food processor and blend until smooth.

Strawberry-Pomegranate Slushie

On hot summer days, this delectable and healthful snack is just what your baby needs.

Prep time: 2 minutes | Cook time: no-cook needed Serves 2

- 1 1/2 cups strawberries, frozen
- 1 cup pomegranate juice

1. Place all the ingredients in a blender and blend until smooth.
2. Serve in a small cup.

Spinach Garbanzo Hummus

Always include greens in your baby's meals. Spinach in garbanzo hummus is delicious. You can double this recipe to share your baby's snack.

Prep time: 4 minutes | Cook time: no-cook needed | Serves 2

- 1 cup baby spinach, fresh
- 1 (15-oz) can garbanzo beans
- 2 tbsp parmesan cheese, grated
- 1/4 cup olive oil
- 1 clove garlic
- 1 tbsp lemon juice

1. Drain the garbanzo beans and rinse well.
2. Put all the ingredients in a blender and blend until desired consistency is reached.
3. Serve with teething biscuit.

Yogurt and Berry Swirl

A tasty way to add dairy to your 9- to 12-month-diet. old's Avoid flavors and sweets in plain yogurt.

Prep time: 5 minutes | Cook time: 5 minutes | Serves 2

- 1 cup blueberries, frozen or fresh
- 1 cup raspberries, frozen or fresh
- 1 whole milk yogurt, plain

1. Place the berries in a blender or food processor and blend until smooth.
2. Set the pan on medium-high heat and simmer the berry Purée for about 5 minutes until it becomes slightly thickened. Stirring occasionally.
3. Serve with a bowl of yogurt and top with berry Purée.

Apricot and Banana Yogurt

Apricots and bananas make fantastic snacks and Purées. Both provide vitamins and minerals your growing infant needs.

Prep time: 2 minutes | Cook time: 3 minutes | Serves 1

- 4 dried apricots, chopped
- 3 tbsp water
- 2 tbsp whole milk yogurt, plain
- 1 banana, medium

1. Cook the dried apricots in a pan with water over low heat. Simmer for 2 – 3 minutes.
2. Place all the ingredients in a food processor and Purée until smooth.
3. Serve in a cup or bowl with baby spoon.

Cantaloupe Purée with Yogurt

Stage 3 baby meal or snack. Creamy cantaloupe with banana and yogurt is great for adults.

Prep time: 1 minute | Cook time: no-cook needed | Serves 6

- 1 cup cantaloupe
- 1/3 cup banana
- 1/4 cup plain Greek yogurt

1. Cut the cantaloupe into two and scoop out the flesh. Peel and slice the banana.
2. In a blender or food processor, place all the ingredients and Purée until smooth.

Frozen Fruit Pops

This dish is great for stage 3 teething babies. This delightful frozen treat contains vitamins and minerals for your baby.

Prep time: 5 minutes | Cook time: no-cook needed | Serves 3

- Mango - Carrot:
- 1/4 cup mango, cubed
- 1/2 cup carrots, grated
- 1.7-oz apple juice
- Berry - Banana:
- 1/4 cup blueberries
- 1/4 cup banana, sliced
- 1 tbsp plain yogurt
- 2 tbsp apple juice
- Strawberry - Yogurt:
- 1/2 cup strawberries
- 1 tbsp plain yogurt
- 1 tbsp apple juice

1. Choose your desired fruit combination. Place all the ingredients in a blender or food processor and blend until smooth.
2. Pour into child safe popsicle molds and freeze for 6 hours.

Tropical Smoothie

Quickly blend together these four ingredients for a smooth and delicious smoothie.

Prep time: 0 min | Cook time: no-cook needed |Serves 3 – 4

- 1 cup coconut milk
- 1/3 cup Greek yogurt, plain
- 1 banana
- 1 cup pineapple, cubed
- 1 cup ice

1. Place all the ingredients in a blender and blend until smooth.
2. For 12 months baby and up, you may opt to add 2 tbsp of honey or agave.

Green Smoothie

An excellent way to convince your toddler to consume a whole cup of spinach is to sneak it into a smoothie.

Prep time: 10 minutes | Cook time: no-cook needed |Serves 4

- 1 cup baby spinach
- 1/2 cup yogurt, plain
- 1/2 avocado
- 1/2 banana
- 1/4 cup formula milk or breast milk (or regular milk if 12 months)
- 1 cup mango, frozen
- 1/4 cup peach, frozen

1. Fresh fruits can be used in this recipe. Just cut the mango and peach into cubes and freeze overnight.
2. Add the first 5 ingredients in a high-speed blender and blend until smooth.
3. Add in the frozen fruits and pulse until combined.
4. Serve with a spoon or in a cup.

Orange-Banana Smoothie

Orange banana smoothie has 3 ingredients. You can substitute whole-milk for homemade curd or yogurt.

Prep time: 3 minutes | Cook time: 5 minutes | Serves 4

- 1/2 cup banana, peeled and sliced
- 1/2 orange, juiced
- 2 tbsp thick curd or yogurt or milk

1. Cut the orange into two and extract the juice to make 2 tbsp, about 1/2 of the fruit. Set aside.
2. Slice the banana and place in a blender along with the curd and orange juice.
3. Blend until smooth.

Blueberry and Mango Smoothie

Your child can eat this for breakfast or dessert. Wheat germ is a simple technique to enhance baby's nutrition.

Prep time: 2 minutes | Cook time: no-cook needed | Serves 8

- 1/4 cup blueberries
- 1/4 cup mango
- 2 tbsp plain Greek yogurt
- 1 tbsp wheat germ

1. Wash the blueberries. Discard the peel of mango and scoop out the flesh.
2. Place all the ingredients in a blender or food processor. Purée until it becomes smooth.

Avocado-Berry-Banana Smoothie

This stunning purple purée is not only simple to prepare, but also packed with healthful ingredients.

Prep time: 5 minutes | Cook time: no-cook needed | serving: 1

- 1/4 avocado
- 1/4 cup blueberries
- 1/2 banana
- 1/4 cup baby oatmeal
- 1/4 cup whole milk yogurt
- 1 tsp flaxseed meal
- 1/4 cup water
- 2 – 3 ice cubes

1. In a high-speed blender, add all the ingredients and blend until smooth.
2. Serve in a cup or bowl with baby spoon.

Appendix 1 Measurement Conversion Chart

Volume Equivalents (Dry)	
US STANDARD	METRIC (APPROXIMATE)
1/8 teaspoon	0.5 mL
1/4 teaspoon	1 mL
1/2 teaspoon	2 mL
3/4 teaspoon	4 mL
1 teaspoon	5 mL
1 tablespoon	15 mL
1/4 cup	59 mL
1/2 cup	118 mL
3/4 cup	177 mL
1 cup	235 mL
2 cups	475 mL
3 cups	700 mL
4 cups	1 L

Volume Equivalents (Liquid)		
US STANDARD	US STANDARD (OUNCES)	METRIC (APPROXIMATE)
2 tablespoons	1 fl.oz.	30 mL
1/4 cup	2 fl.oz.	60 mL
1/2 cup	4 fl.oz.	120 mL
1 cup	8 fl.oz.	240 mL
1 1/2 cup	12 fl.oz.	355 mL
2 cups or 1 pint	16 fl.oz.	475 mL
4 cups or 1 quart	32 fl.oz.	1 L
1 gallon	128 fl.oz.	4 L

Temperatures Equivalents	
FAHRENHEIT(F)	CELSIUS(CAPPROXIMATE)
225 °F	107 °C
250 °F	120 ° °C
275 °F	135 °C
300 °F	150 °C
325 °F	160 °C
350 °F	180 °C
375 °F	190 °C
400 °F	205 °C
425 °F	220 °C
450 °F	235 °C
475 °F	245 °C
500 °F	260 °C

Weight Equivalents	
US STANDARD	METRIC (APPROXIMATE)
1 ounce	28 g
2 ounces	57 g
5 ounces	142 g
10 ounces	284 g
15 ounces	425 g
16 ounces (1 pound)	455 g
1.5 pounds	680 g
2 pounds	907 g

Appendix 2 The Dirty Dozen and Clean Fifteen

The Environmental Working Group (EWGis a nonprofit, nonpartisan organization dedicated to protecting human health and the environment Its mission is to empower people to live healthier lives in a healthier environment. This organization publishes an annual list of the twelve kinds of produce, in sequence, that have the highest amount of pesticide residue-the Dirty Dozen-as well as a list of the fifteen kinds ofproduce that have the least amount of pesticide residue-the Clean Fifteen.

THE DIRTY DOZEN	
The 2016 Dirty Dozen includes the following produce. These are considered among the year's most important produce to buy organic:	
Strawberries	Spinach
Apples	Tomatoes
Nectarines	Bell peppers
Peaches	Cherry tomatoes
Celery	Cucumbers
Grapes	Kale/collard greens
Cherries	Hot peppers

The Dirty Dozen list contains two additional itemskale/collard greens and hot peppers-because they tend to contain trace levels of highly hazardous pesticides.

THE CLEAN FIFTEEN	
The least critical to buy organically are the Clean Fifteen list. The following are on the 2016 list:	
Avocados	Papayas
Corn	Kiw
Pineapples	Eggplant
Cabbage	Honeydew
Sweet peas	Grapefruit
Onions	Cantaloupe
Asparagus	Cauliflower
Mangos	

Some of the sweet corn sold in the United States are made from genetically engineered (GEseedstock. Buy organic varieties of these crops to avoid GE produce.

Appendix 3 Index

LUCIA L. DAVIS

CPSIA information can be obtained
at www.ICGtesting.com
Printed in the USA
BVHW011531251122
652756BV00004B/299